THE COMPLETE GUIDE TO PLANNING YOUR ESTATE

A Step-By-Step Plan to Protect Your Assets, Limit Your Taxes, and Ensure Your Wishes Are Fulfilled

By Sandy Baker

THE COMPLETE GUIDE TO PLANNING YOUR ESTATE:
A Step-by-Step Plan to Protect Your Assets, Limit Your Taxes, and Ensure Your Wishes Are Fulfilled

Copyright © 2007 by Atlantic Publishing Group, Inc.
1405 SW 6th Ave. • Ocala, Florida 34471 • 800-814-1132 • 352-622-1875–Fax
Web site: www.atlantic-pub.com • E-mail: sales@atlantic-pub.com
SAN Number: 268-1250

ISBN-13: 978-1-60138-049-4   ISBN-10: 1-60138-049-6

Library of Congress Cataloging-in-Publication Data
Baker, Sandy Ann, 1976-
The complete guide to planning your estate : a step-by-step plan to protect your assets, limit your taxes, and ensure your wishes are fulfilled / by Sandy Baker.
     p. cm.
Includes bibliographical references.
ISBN-13: 978-1-60138-049-4 (alk. paper)
ISBN-10: 1-60138-049-6 (alk. paper)
1. Estate planning--United States. 2. Estates (Law)--United States. I. Title.

    KF750.Z9B35 2007
    346.7305′2--dc22
                    2007022410

EDITOR: Tracie Kendzoira • tkendzoira@atlantic-pub.com
PROOFREADER: Vickie Taylor • vtaylor@atlantic-pub.com

Printed in the United States

Printed on Recycled Paper

We recently lost our beloved pet "Bear," who was not only our best and dearest friend but also the "Vice President of Sunshine" here at Atlantic Publishing. He did not receive a salary but worked tirelessly 24 hours a day to please his parents. Bear was a rescue dog that turned around and showered myself, my wife Sherri, his grandparents Jean, Bob and Nancy and every person and animal he met (maybe not rabbits) with friendship and love. He made a lot of people smile every day.

We wanted you to know that a portion of the profits of this book will be donated to The Humane Society of the United States.

–Douglas & Sherri Brown

THE HUMANE SOCIETY
OF THE UNITED STATES ©

The human-animal bond is as old as human history. We cherish our animal companions for their unconditional affection and acceptance. We feel a thrill when we glimpse wild creatures in their natural habitat or in our own backyard.

Unfortunately, the human-animal bond has at times been weakened. Humans have exploited some animal species to the point of extinction.

The Humane Society of the United States makes a difference in the lives of animals here at home and worldwide. The HSUS is dedicated to creating a world where our relationship with animals is guided by compassion. We seek a truly humane society in which animals are respected for their intrinsic value, and where the human-animal bond is strong.

Want to help animals? We have plenty of suggestions. Adopt a pet from a local shelter, join The Humane Society and be a part of our work to help companion animals and wildlife. You will be funding our educational, legislative, investigative and outreach projects in the U.S. and across the globe.

Or perhaps you'd like to make a memorial donation in honor of a pet, friend or relative? You can through our Kindred Spirits program. And if you'd like to contribute in a more structured way, our Planned Giving Office has suggestions about estate planning, annuities, and even gifts of stock that avoid capital gains taxes.

Maybe you have land that you would like to preserve as a lasting habitat for wildlife. Our Wildlife Land Trust can help you. Perhaps the land you want to share is a backyard—that's enough. Our Urban Wildlife Sanctuary Program will show you how to create a habitat for your wild neighbors.

So you see, it's easy to help animals. And The HSUS is here to help.

The Humane Society of the United States
2100 L Street NW
Washington, DC 20037
202-452-1100
www.hsus.org

CONTENTS

———

CHAPTER 6: WILL SUBSTITUTIONS THAT SAVE

FOREWORD

"I love my family, and I do not want to leave them with a mess." Most people wish that there was a way to prevent burdening their loved ones when they die, and yet creating a burden is exactly what they do. If you do not prepare a well thought out estate plan in case of incapacity or death, the state where you live has one already set up for you. But unlike a professionally prepared plan, this one will be the most expensive, time consuming, difficult, public, and aggravating one that exists.

Under this plan, your county probate court judge will appoint an administrator (usually a probate attorney, maybe even a campaign contributor for his re-election) to contact your relatives and creditors to settle your estate. This process could take between one and three years, sometimes more, cost between five and ten percent of your estate, and all the information you thought was private will now be public record. There will even be an additional charge against your estate every time the probate attorney talks on the telephone about your estate or pays bills to one of your creditors with your money.

If you are alive and physically or mentally incapacitated, the same probate judge will appoint someone (again, it could be that probate attorney) to act as your legal guardian to make sure your bills get paid, you receive proper medical treatment, and your physical needs for food, clothing, and shelter are met. Every time that attorney does anything for you, he or she will charge you a bill at his or her typical hourly rate of between $100 and $500, easily resulting in a cost of up to and over $20,000 per year while the guardianship is in effect. This is in addition to your bills that will be paid for with your money. The trouble does not stop there, however, because if you later regain your capacity, you cannot simply walk into the probate judge's office and declare that you are ready to take over again. Instead, you must formally petition the probate court to prove your legal competence to remove the legal guardianship. However, just because you think you are competent does not necessarily mean that the probate judge will agree. The probate judge will most likely err on the side of caution and keep the guardianship in effect indefinitely.

The attorney who represents the guardianship will not be inclined to lose those legal fees and will probably petition the probate court to keep the guardianship in effect. That attorney will tell you it is in your best interest, but instead it will be in the attorney's best interest. So now you will have to hire a *second* attorney to petition the probate court to remove the guardianship. Both attorneys will be paid for with your money.

This book goes though the best methods to avoid these messes and make sure you have an estate plan that will serve you and your loved ones' needs. It explains, in simple and easy to understand terms, topics including wills, trusts, durable powers of attorney, living wills, probate by-pass methods, who the professionals are, and how they can help you. It is a great read, and I recommend it to anyone who wants to avoid a mess.

David J. Bernstein
Attorney at Law
www.estatefacts.com

INTRODUCTION

Your estate is what you have worked to develop. You deserve to make decisions about your property and your money.

Using this book as a guide, with its easy to understand language, you will learn how to plan your estate legally.

With a will in hand and a plan for your estate, you can be assured that your wishes will be met and that you have taken the steps to:

- Protect your loved ones from taxes that can literally take most of your estate.

- Give your favorite charities the funds you want them to have.

- Save your survivors from making decisions about your estate.

- Provide for your loved ones.

An estimated 60 percent of people die without a will or any type of estate plan. That means that the government settles the estate, and if there are no clearly defined heirs, the state takes everything.

Your estate plan is a living document that changes with you. As your life moves forward, your estate plan can provide for life changes. By getting your wishes down on paper now, you take care of everyone who is important to you no matter what happens so that they have the funds they need to live without you.

This simple, easy to follow book will help you to understand each step of the estate process and allow you to protect those you love.

1

AN INTRODUCTION TO ESTATE PLANNING

WHY DO ALL THIS WORK?

If you want to decide what happens to your money and possessions, you need to do it through your estate plan.

When you do plan your estate, you can do several important things:

1. Because of a rising divorce rate, the normal family today includes numbers of people whom the government will not take into consideration when examining your estate.

2. You cut or eliminate the amount the government takes from your loved ones.

3. You protect your business. An estate plan can help the business stay open and thriving.

WHAT IS AN ESTATE?

Often, people think they do not have enough of an estate to have to worry about planning. But if you have a home, credit card debt, or heirs, you need to plan your estate. Your estate consists of everything that belongs to you. Here are some items that come into play when planning your estate:

- Actual money: This includes cash that you may have, checking, and savings accounts.

- Certificates of deposit.

- Your portfolio: stocks, mutual funds, and bonds.

- Your retirement funds: pension funds, 401(k), your IRAs, and any other money that has been reserved for retirement.

- Your house, your vehicles, and all property inside your home, including clothing, furniture, appliances, your jewelry, and other valuables.

- Insurance products: life insurance, especially.

- Your business: any funds or ownership of your business.

- Annuities that you may have coming to you.

- Anything else that you have that you consider valuable either sentimentally or monetarily.

One important note is that your estate planning will likely include both positive and negative balance amounts. For example, it will include all the items listed above as positive balances, provided they do not carry a loan or a negative balance. Your mortgage on your home may be a negative balance because you still owe money on it. In addition to these things, money that you owe others, taxes that you owe, and any credit that you have outstanding is also a negative balance.

Even though these things may carry a negative balance, they too need to be planned into your estate. It is essential to know this information to figure out your estate's actual worth.

℘ Case Study: Janice Engelberth ℘

What is the most important thing for others to consider, based on your experience, when it comes to planning an estate?

Learn about the taxes that are due for the estate and when they are due.

My husband's health did not allow him to sign documents, and even though I had the power of attorney, I could not sign his name on real estate documents. I made sure there was one bank account with the minimum amount kept in it for cashing government checks, and I found that process to be a challenge too.

If one is able, prepay funeral expenses so that this burden does not happen later.

I also found that it was important to make sure that all people involved have a medical directive as this could be a potential problem when something happens. We established all these things in an effort to make the process after death easier.

When you completed the process, did you feel secure?

Yes, I did feel like I was in a better place for whatever comes. It was worth the effort to know that everything was planned. We worked through a lawyer who specialized in trusts. Before, we had almost all our holdings in joint ownership accounts. In 2000 each of us had a trust. In 2006 it was revised because of health issues. We wanted to sell real estate, and he could not write his name to sign the documents. If we had not had the trust, our four children would have had to sell property quickly to pay the almost $250,000 in taxes that would be due.

Janice Engelberth
Warsaw, IN

What Is Your Estate Worth?

It is simple math to figure out what your estate is worth. Start by adding all the positive items together for the value of your assets.

Next, subtract the amount of money that you owe from this asset balance. The balance is the value of your assets.

The value of your estate will change over time.

If you own a business, for example, you will need to know the value of the business itself, all equipment, and the value of your stock.

Any money or property that will be yours in the future may need to be included in your estate as well.

What Goes into Estate Planning?

Property Types

There are several different types of property that should be included in your estate. The most common is that of real property, including any type of real estate that you may own, such as a timeshare and any improvements you have made to the land you own.

Personal property is broken down into two types. One is tangible personal property, which is any type of property that you can touch. Examples are clothing and furniture.

The other type of personal property is intangible, including your money, your bank accounts, and your stock certificates. It includes anything that is financially oriented that belongs to you.

Property Interest: Defined

The two types of property interest include legal interest and beneficial interest.

Legal interest means that you only have a legal right to the property, but you do not have the ability to use it. One example is a trust. If you are the trustee of property that belongs to someone else, you get to make decisions about how that property is used, but you do not get to use those funds or property for your own benefit. As a trustee, you make decisions about the money but cannot touch the funds for your own use.

The second type of property interest is beneficial interest. Here, you do have the benefit from the property, meaning that you do have use of and the right to the property. There are two additional types of interest that are defined as beneficial:

- **Present interest:** In this type of interest, you have the right to use the interest right now, as you see fit. Here, there is no wait to get the benefits from your property.

- **Future interest:** As the name describes, you have the benefit coming to you in the future. This type of interest can be further broken down:

  ○ Vested interest is the benefit that you get in future interest that allows you to do anything you want with no strings attached.

  ○ Contingent interest is the benefit that you will get only if you abide by the rules set forth.

WHO WILL HELP YOU PLAN YOUR ESTATE

While you can do all your estate planning yourself, it is better to use some key people along the way to help you to make the most of estate planning. Each one plays their own role in helping you to get your estate set up with a plan for its future.

You will want to work with four key individuals during this process.

1.) **Estate Planning Attorney:** You will need a good estate planning attorney or an attorney that you know and trust. Having someone whose specialty is estate planning makes the best sense.

2.) **Accountant:** You need an accountant to help you determine value and manage taxes on your estate, one who can help you make the right decisions now to avoid costly taxes later on.

3.) **Financial Planner:** A financial planner, who helps you make decisions regarding investments and other finances, will also be needed. You may consult with a financial planner for guidance only or turn over investment and management of your estate.

4.) **Insurance Agent:** You need the help of an insurance agent because you will want to give your family protection. The obvious benefit here is life insurance, but you should also consider disability insurance as well as liability insurance.

A CLOSER LOOK: THE ATTORNEY

An attorney should be able to look at your situation and prepare for possible scenarios. What if you die before you get married but you still want all your belongings to go to your fiancé? What if your heir dies before you do? All these (and countless more) situations are something that your attorney needs to plan out for you.

Ask your attorney to provide you with the legal advice necessary in handling trusts, wills, your business, and every aspect of your estate planning.

What to Look for in an Attorney

You should look for these qualities in the attorney you plan to hire:

- You should look for an attorney that specializes in estate planning. What experience does he or she have that will serve your needs? Ask about the person's legal experience in your area and with people whose financial situation is similar to yours. What amount of dedication and time can your attorney give you?

- Can you trust the attorney? You want someone that you feel has your best interests at heart and who is working for you. You also should like them because you will be dealing with them for some time to come.

A CLOSER LOOK: THE FINANCIAL PLANNER

If you think that financial planners have the sole job of helping people make money, you are wrong. The financial planner has the job of helping you make your financial dreams come true and to give you the advice that you need to manage your funds over the course of your lifetime. With a financial planner, you will be able to provide for your loved ones when you are gone.

It is important to determine the role of your planner. Some people want to find someone they can trust, give them a fixed amount of money per month to manage investments, and watch their numbers rise. Others want only to be told how to handle their funds, as in which investments are a good choice and then make the decisions themselves. You could be some place in the middle too and inform your planner.

What to Look for in a Financial Planner

For most people, it is important to take into consideration who they will be working with. You need to find someone you can trust and someone that you know will have your best interests at heart. To do that, consider these tips for finding a financial planner that is right for you.

- Who is he or she?

- Where did he or she learn his or her trade?

- What credentials does he or she have that will fit with what you need and want from him or her?

- What is his or her background, and how does it relate to what you need?

- What does he or she do? One thing that is essential to take note of is the fact that financial planners are all different. Our recommendation is to find a Certified Financial Planner, also called a CFP. To be a CFP, they must pass an exam to become licensed. This follows a long list of financial training courses at the college level. In addition, he or she will need to have at least three years of experience working with financial planning clients. While there are many other types of financial planners out there, you want one that has the title to go along with the skills he or she says he or she has.

- How does he or she get paid? It is important to determine this based on the financial planners you are considering. Those that get a commission from the products that they are telling you that you must have are not the best way to go. Look for those that are paid a fee only or those that are paid based on how well your portfolio does. Make sure you clearly understand if the financial planner is getting paid to sell you a product.

✐ Case Study: William Russo ✐

In consideration of the timeliness of starting estate planning, the best time is now. Each time you title an account or designate a beneficiary, you are estate planning. Each person/couple needs to evaluate their current situation and how they want their estate to be distributed if something were to

✍ Case Study: William Russo ✍

happen to him or her. If his or her children are under 18, would he or she want the executor and guardian to make decisions as to how and when his or her children get access to his or her estate? These decisions need to be made now, not at a later date. Nobody knows what tomorrow brings.

Boomers need to make sure that their retirement assets are set up in a manner that their heirs have tax favorable access to the retirement accounts. This means knowing whether it is better to leave assets in company plans or rolling them over to IRAs. Planning now insures that if something were to happen to you, your heirs will be taken care of with the estate while minimizing the tax exposure.

The job of the financial planner is to make people take the time to identify their goals, educate them as to the options available, and to make sure that recommendations are followed through. Once a plan is implemented, then ongoing review ensures that the plan is modified to take into account changes that occur.

A person should expect to spend an hour to an hour and a half discussing his or her current situations (net worth, spending plan), goals and priorities, time frames, and what is important to him or her and why. What got him or her to this point, what has worked, what has not, what other professionals do they work with, and what outcomes does he or she desire to make him or her feel the relationship is worthwhile, all will be discussed.

My job can only be successful if there is a level of trust and all information that affects his or her financial affairs is disclosed. This is mutual, as I must be able to convey a level of trust before anyone would feel comfortable disclosing his or her financial affairs, thoughts, and concerns.

☙ Case Study: William Russo ❧

A financial planner is a good investment because he or she is an independent entity that can provide objective insight into a person's financial affairs. A planner should never tell a client what he or she wants to hear, but should explain to him or her the impact of decisions that are made on his or her financial plan. We try to make sure people understand that to build wealth they must first spend less than they earn. We see to it that clients commit to and follow a sound, long-term investment strategy. We reinforce the need to stay disciplined and exercise patience.

William Russo, CFP
33595 Bainbridge Road, Suite 104
Solon, Ohio 44139
Phone: 440-349-4980
Brusso@concordfinancialplan.com
www.concordfinancialplan.com

A CLOSER LOOK: THE ACCOUNTANT

The accountant is a key player on the team of estate planning, and you should insure that he or she has what it takes to provide you with the help you need. Your accountant's job is to help you to see how the tax side of estate planning will work. As you will see later in this book, taxes can be the death of your estate. But, if you make decisions now regarding them, you can steer your investments and your estate away from any costly problems.

Think of the accountant that is hired for a business (maybe even your own). He or she has the job of helping the business to manage its money, to do its tax returns, and to tell it where they stand at any one point. In addition, the accountant looks at the investments being made and helps you make decisions regarding taxes in the future. He or she may tell you that if you invest X amount of dollars into upgrading equipment that you can claim it as a deduction. The same scenario is true for your accountant on the estate planning team you are building.

The accountant will work with you to determine where you stand right now and where you are headed. He or she may suggest a few changes now so that down the road you can avoid some costly mistakes. Or he or she may be able to keep you on top of the latest changes in tax laws regarding your estate. One of the key things he or she can help with is telling you how to give "financial gifts" so that they benefit you.

What to Look for in an Accountant

The accountant is a primary role player, and therefore, you should have some clear cut goals for him or her when it comes to estate planning. Here are some things to look for in a qualified accountant:

- Is he or she a CPA? You want to insure that the accountant you select is a Certified Public Accountant. This means that he or she has taken the necessary educational steps toward earning a license from the American Institute of Certified Public Accountants, which is a rather difficult thing to do.

- Who is he or she working for? You should ensure that the accountant you hire is not working for anyone that could encourage him or her to sell you products that you do not necessarily need. You can easily learn this just by asking him or her.

- What experience does he or she have working on estate planning? This is key because many CPAs will have a specialty field, and just because he or she knows how to do estate planning accounting does not necessarily mean he or she knows all there is to know about it. You want someone that can provide you with a specialty in estate planning.

Taking the time necessary to find these traits can pay off right away. A good accountant can meet with you to discuss the changes needed to be made quickly and begin working on a strategy with you to improve your tax burden down the road. You will save money in the long-term by investing in an accountant now.

A CLOSER LOOK: THE INSURANCE AGENT

The final piece of the puzzle of estate planning is your insurance agent. It is important to know just what he or she can offer you in regards to estate planning. We will go into more detail about life insurance and other insurance products, but for now realize the importance of getting someone on board to help with these decisions.

The difference with an insurance agent is that he or she is looking to sell you products. A good one will help you to wade through the different options until you find something that works for your particular needs, but some will also try to convince you of purchasing things you do not have a need for. What is important is finding someone you can trust.

You should have an insurance agent on your estate planning team if and when you have:

- Dependants

- A spouse

- Children

- Anyone that will need some protection and help if and when you pass away

These conditions are likely to change over time. Insurance is like a blanket of protection that you can throw over your loved ones in times of trouble.

While money cannot solve everything, it will help a family to survive a catastrophic event, such as your premature death.

What to Look for in an Insurance Agent

You may already have an insurance agent handling your automobile insurance or your house insurance. If you like and trust these individuals, and their company offers the types of insurance that you need, by all means work with them. Otherwise, before you select a new insurance agent, ask the following questions:

- What is his or her experience? In the field of insurance agents, you need to find out what he or she can help you with when it comes to estate planning tools. An insurance agent should offer a wide range of life insurance, disability insurance, and liability insurance products. He or she should also be willing and capable of helping you to find a product that meets your needs.

- Do you trust him or her? You should find an insurance agent that you can trust. Sometimes, there is someone that has been in the family for years and you want to use them. Do so, but only if they are a comparable choice to others out there. You need to know that when you purchase a product it is what you think it is. The insurance agent should make time for you, too, and that means explaining every last detail that you do not understand.

- Is what he or she is offering cost effective? There is a range in price when it comes to insurance products. You may want to consider looking at several agents that fit into the above categories that can provide you with the best rate. This means looking at the short- and long-term of each of your goals.

Finding the right agent is a must for estate planning. The good news is that many are more than willing to help you.

GETTING STARTED WITH YOUR ESTATE PLANNING

Now that you know what it means and what it takes to plan your estate, you can move into the process of making it happen.

There are many ways that you can do this, and you can even hire someone to do it all for you. Nevertheless, it is your job to see it through from beginning to end. The process itself is just that, a process. You cannot possibly get it all figured out in a heartbeat, and it will take days, weeks, and even months to come to fruition. The good news is that the end result is well worth the process that it takes to get there.

The normal process of setting up an estate plan is what you should be following. You do need to invest time in making each step happen but you need to have a clearly defined path to making that come true. If you read this book and say, "I have to do these things," and never put your hand to it, then you will not realize your goals.

What makes it even more challenging to many is the fact that it takes time to work through each step. If you go to set up a trust and find that you need to fill out some additional paperwork, get some signatures, and then find that there may be another route that is better … you change paths, get frustrated, and eventually just do not move through the process. For this reason, you need to establish a mentality of getting the job done.

Here, we will reveal a few things to put your mind to now, to get you started. In each chapter of this book, you will find the details that you need to bring together each step in the process.

YOUR METHOD FOR SUCCESS

Here is an example of the plan to get you from not having an estate plan to having one that completely fills your needs. Will you make it there? If you follow these steps, you are sure to make it to the summit.

Step 1: What Are Your Goals?

You sat down with this book for a reason. It may be that you are trying to figure out how to help your elderly parents, or you may be concerned about what could happen to your family if you were to die suddenly. Your goals are likely to be situated around these things. No matter what your goals are, you should have them in mind while working on your estate planning.

What is it that you want to accomplish by having an estate plan in place?

- Protecting your spouse if you die?

- Helping your children pay for college?

- Helping to protect your home and investments?

- Making your wishes come true?

- Insuring that you have the funds to manage a life that you want to live?

Take the time right now to stop reading and to write down your goals. This is something that you should take pencil and paper to, because when the waters get cloudy and confusing during estate planning, you will be able to come back and say, "This is what my goal is."

Step 2: Get Your Team Situated

As we mentioned, it is important to get professionals working for you. Believe it or not, this step in the process may take you a few extra weeks to complete. To choose those that are best suited for your needs, you should be comparing several. For example, if you are going to be looking for an insurance agent, talk to several and find out what they can offer you. Plan to meet with these individuals and get a feel for what they can do to serve your needs.

Eventually, you will want to select the person that has the best outlook for your lifestyle and needs, but also the one that you seem to work the best with. If you do not like his or her personality, are you going to call them when you have a question about something?

Hiring people to help you plan your estate is one of the smartest decisions you can make. You want to find others that are willing to help you through the process, step by step, and are in it for the long-term.

Finally, make sure your team is working together. You want your attorney to be able to contact your accountant and let him know about a new plan that may be working. Likewise, your financial planner may suggest a new investment, but your accountant may be leery because of the tax implications that it has. Getting them to work together can be one of the best moves you make.

Step 3: Do Your Homework

As much as you did not like doing homework while you were in school, it is now more important than ever to have the information that you need to make the right decisions, and homework is the best way to do it.

Although you are hiring people to help you develop an estate plan, you are still the leader of the team, and therefore, you need to make sure that all the right moves are being made. To get started, learn where you stand right now and what you can do to improve to the position that you would like to be at. For example, you want to ensure that your financial investments are working for you right now, in the long- and short-term. You want to ensure that if you have a will, it is completely up to date on your current situation.

You should do your own research on the benefits of estate planning and which products are best for you. Just purchasing this book is one of the best tools that you have available to you. Keeping yourself educated about the options and new laws, taxes and scandals that are out there helps you to keep yourself on the path to having an ideal estate plan.

Step 4: Develop and Implement an Action Plan

Many times during business management courses you will hear about the action plan. You may cringe at the number of times that you have had to write these and you may have thought them to be ridiculous. But look back at the number of times that they have helped you. Now, implement this into your current life and your estate planning needs.

Develop a plan of how you will accomplish your goals. You may schedule a time to work out the important qualifications of the trusts you want to set up. As you can see, there is quite a bit to do. See the following example:

✍ Estate Goal Plan ✍	
Week 1	Work on and finish creating my will
Week 2	Meet with my lawyer to secure the details of my will
Week 3	Meet with my financial planner to determine investments for the future

✍ Estate Goal Plan ✍	
Week 4	Meet with my accountant to talk about gifts that will help me with my taxes

Again, this book will take you through much of this. However, what you need do to now is to implement these goals. Read through this book; determine what your goals are and what you need to do. Then, implement them by going through the book a second time, this time moving forward only when you have made leeway on the current goals on which you are working.

Your action plan should be something that motivates you, too. Think of the relief you will have knowing that your family is well taken care of. Think of the benefits you will gain just by working with a financial planner to get your finances in order. If you feel the need, allow yourself a reward for accomplishing these important tasks.

Develop a plan of when you will work on your estate plan, how you will get the plan accomplished, including a time table for progress, and what you want to make happen. Implement this by doing what you say you need to do.

Hold yourself accountable for the action plan, too. If you decide to work on the plan five hours per week, then do so. Although it sounds morbid, none of us knows if we have another 60 years or two weeks to live. Dedicating time to getting your estate plan complete is a must.

Step 5: Come Back to It

The one mistake that many people make is that of planning out their estate only to forget about it. Unfortunately, your estate is not something that will stay the same throughout the course of your life, nor will what you put into your plan remain the same. Because of this, you will need to come back and revisit the key issues of your estate plan to ensure that it provides you with the utmost protection and the clearest goals to how your life is being lived right now, not how it was lived before.

Many people make a will and then forget about it. When he or she dies, his or her heirs are insulted because their ex-wife or their fourth unexpected child was not included in the will. Or there may be additional property that does not get figured into it because you never updated it. Each of these things can cause problems for you down the road.

The good news is that with a good estate planning attorney, he or she should be willing to revisit your will yearly (including all your estate plans) and update them as necessary. Perhaps every year around your birthday you want to plan some time to look over what is in place and make decisions about it if needed.

This does not have to be a long, drawn out process. Just picking up the finished plans and looking at them is better than tucking them into a safety deposit box and forgetting about them. Life changes every day and you need to ensure that the information in your estate plan is current.

ARE YOU READY?

It is essential to the well-being of your estate planning that you take each step of the process seriously. You should commit to spending time looking at what you need to do, deciding on the right solution to the problem, and implementing it. We will help take you through each of those steps, in detail.

You should also take heart in the fact that planning an estate does take time. If you or someone you love is in need of a fast solution, contact an estate planning attorney right away; this can help to speed up the process. In critical times, it is essential to implement fast decisions, but that does not mean that those decisions cannot be made with thorough careful consideration.

Now, it is time to begin your journey. Once you have gotten your team together, take into consideration the steps provided in this book.

2

WHAT ARE YOU WORTH?

As part of the estate planning process, you will need to protect the possessions that you have. But, if you do not know how much you have or even what you have, that can be challenging.

In this chapter, we will look at the need and the process of calculating just what your estate is worth. Believe it or not, you may find yourself surprised at your value. Most people do not realize what needs to go into their estate, and therefore, make the mistake of not including everything that they have that has value to it. Mind you, we are not talking about determining who will get the shirt you are wearing or the pencil in your desk drawer. Rather, we are talking about items that have some sort of worth to them.

Most people think they know what they are worth. But most people are far off from an accurate picture of that worth. This can be costly when it comes time to plan your estate because you may not take into account some items or even worse, you may fail to manage the tax deductions or costs that those items may have. That could be a real problem for you, ultimately.

In addition to this, you may have some debt. Big or small, this too factors into your worth, and you must take into consideration just what that is and how it affects virtually every aspect of your estate plan.

The trick of estate planning is realizing that things change over time. If you are smart, you are planning your estate well before you reach old age. But even when you get into the midst of it, you will still find that things change. The value of your estate changes significantly over time. This too must be taken into consideration today as well as in the future.

All these things need to be taken into consideration when it comes to estate planning. You need to have a foundation for success by planning your estate based on what you own, what you owe, and what changes will happen in the future.

Look at the various types of real property that you have and determine what it is worth.

WHAT IS YOUR HOME WORTH?

To get started, you need to consider your real property. Real property is the type of property that is tangible, including your home, for example. For most people, the home is the most valuable asset that he or she owns in real property. Yet, do you know what your home is worth?

Unless you have purchased your home recently, you do not have a good understanding of the value that it has. That is because the value of your home has fluctuated just as the real estate markets have moved quite a bit in the last several years.

In some areas, market values for homes have increased by leaps and bounds over the last ten or so years, yet there is a slight cooling off happening now. Even if you read this book ten years from now, you still will have seen ups and downs in the market, all which play a significant role in the value of your property.

In order to determine the value of your home, you need to do a bit of research. One of the best ways to understand the value of your home is to have a property appraiser come to your home and price it for you. This person's job is to know the value of the home. It is his or her job to compare your home to others in the area and what they have sold for over the last six months to a year. The appraiser will look at the size and details, and will walk through your home looking for benefits and disadvantages in order to get an accurate price for it. In addition, he or she will need to provide you with a good estimate of what you could get for your home if you sold it today.

The largest drawback to using an appraiser to do this work is that it will cost you somewhere between $250 up to $500 or more in some areas. This cost is something you should consider taking on, especially when you need to know an accurate price for your home so that you can split it between your loved ones.

If you do not want to go this route, find a quality, experienced real estate agent and talk to them. He or she can help you determine the value of a home as it would sell by looking solely at what your property features are in comparison to other homes in the area that have sold. He or she may charge you for this service, but it is likely to less expensive than an appraiser. However, you will also find that this is not as accurate of a description of your home's value either.

You can ask for this information and then do the pricing yourself by comparing the homes in your area to your own for similarities. Yet this poses even more of a problem because, unless you know the value of features, the benefits of one neighborhood over the other, or you know the valuation of homes in general, this simply is not going to give you an accurate price for your home.

WHAT OTHER PROPERTY IS OUT THERE?

Do you own any other type of property? Here are three types of real estate ownership situations in which you may already have property and, therefore, have to consider the value of this property for your real property valuation.

> **Timeshare:** Do you own a timeshare? If you have a second home or you own a part of that home, this is considered to be real property and something you need to know the value of. To determine the value of this type of property, you will need to follow the same basic principles as you did for your home's valuation.

> **Real Estate Partnerships:** Do you have a partnership in which you and someone else own property? One such thing is that of a Limited Liability Company (LLC), or Limited Liability Partnerships (LLP). Here, you do not have direct ownership of the property, but you own it through these companies. This is a rather confusing aspect because the value of an LLC can go up and down quite a bit in just a year. In addition, you may be restricted on how and when you can sell it. To determine the value of these, you will need to know its worth based on where it is, what is there, and how these things change over time. You almost always need to have a professional give you the value of it, but you will have to have this type of property reassessed as it changes.

> **Real Estate/Landlord:** Do you own land or property that you rent to others? If so, this is an important piece of your real property. You could own a home that you rent to others or you may own part of an office building. These things play a real role in the financial outlook of your estate and need to be carefully considered. You should have a commercial real estate appraiser look at the value

of your property or, if you know what you are doing, use the net operating income and capitalization rate of your property to determine the value of the land and property.

Land is one of the highest valued items for estate planning, but it is by far not the only real property that you have. In addition to this type of property, you need to know the value of other property that you have.

REAL PROPERTY BEYOND REAL ESTATE

Both tangible and intangible property needs to have its value determined. This could be a process that takes you some time, but nevertheless it must be done. You may want to work with your estate planning attorney in determining the value of some of these items. While we will give you advice on how to do this here, it can fluctuate greatly.

Your personal property ranges greatly in value. Many of the items that you have, such as that pencil on your desk, have little to no value. So, why do you need to bother with tracking those differences? Why do you need to write down all the items that you have?

With estate planning your goal is to provide for your loved ones, and even if you do not believe it, dividing your personal items among them, even the least in value, is a must. Therefore, while you are taking the time to list all your property for valuation needs, you should also be taking the time to list all your property in order to know who will get what.

Here are some steps to help you to determine the best way to work through this:

- Work with your insurance provider. Most homeowner's policies will require that you have a list of the items in your home in order to provide coverage for those items. Therefore, you can do this list one time and have it available for everything you will need it for.

- List each item in your home in categories. To do this, you can use a spreadsheet on your computer or even just a piece of paper. A good way to do this is to go room by room to make the determinations. Start in your bedroom for example, and then move into the living room, etc.

- List items in your bedroom, all of them. Include those that have sentimental value but not real monetary value (photos, the pin handed down from your grandmother), those that have actual value (your furniture, artwork, and jewelry), and those that have no financial value or sentimental value (clothing, the knick knacks that are nothing more than dust collectors).

- Do not spend too much time on those items that have no value, but do spend time tracking the value of items that do have some financial benefit to you. You should write down the estimated value of the item; more on how to do this later.

- Go room by room to take note of everything that is in those rooms that has some value to it. Pay attention to the details that you may not have thought about.

Tips for Valuing Your "Stuff"

Determining the value of your belongings is no doubt going to be a long process. But there are a few ways that you can cut down on the overload of time and get the task done.

First off, determine what the value of each worthy item is. To do this, you can make an estimated guess. If you do not have some type of idea of how much something is worth, you can use the Web to help you. Visit resale shops for additional help, or use online auctions to find out what a product just like yours is selling for. You want to get as close to the actual item as possible, including the age and features, to get an accurate cost.

Another tip that makes the process of valuation faster is doing so with the help of your camera. You can take a picture of the item, figure the costs, and tape it onto the back or even just listing it on a disc. In any case, digital or not, pictures make the process faster. If you have a video recorder, this is even faster and can be just as effective as a piece of paper.

Do Not Forget the Intangible

What we have talked about so far are the things that you can touch. But you have real property that extends beyond this level that needs to be noted. Each product that you have needs to be valuated to determine how it will affect your estate.

For most, intangible property is the most valuable property that they own. And, depending on what you have done throughout the course of your life, it may be the easiest of all your property to valuate, which means that this part of the estate planning process is rather straightforward.

What is this type of property? Do you have stocks, bonds, mutual funds, annuities, savings accounts, or certificates of deposit (CD)? These are just a few of the examples that you need to take into consideration. Here is a check list for you to determine what you have, where it is, and how much it is worth.

1. Determine all your assets that are intangible or money related. List them and list where you have them. For example, you may have a savings account at one bank and a CD at another, or you could have mutual funds that are spread out into several companies. Here, you need a list of where everything is and what it is. It makes sense to pull out all your paperwork and write down your account numbers including the information you need to track the value of the item.

2. For some items you just need to check your statement to know what the value of it is. To see how much you have in your savings account, just check the statement. This can also go for your retirement accounts, your certificates of deposit, or other accounts like this that you may have.

3. If you have a broker that manages your money or investments, then you will want to meet with them to get a breakdown of the value that each investment has. Although you will be using a financial planner to manage your money, you still need to take into consideration what you have right now.

4. Do you have stocks? You can learn their worth just by looking at the market at any given time. You should have a basic knowledge of the worth of each share and total shares that you have. You can also do this with mutual funds that you own. You can find them listed online or in your local newspaper.

5. Interest payment schedules are also important for assets that have a long-term interest plan — for example, your savings account. Even more so, if you have a savings bond that will gradually increase in value, you will need to know what that increase is, both in what the value of the product is now and what it will be in the years to come.

What other products do you have and if you were to sell them today, what value would they bring to you? These things are critical to know and taking the steps right now to determine them will benefit you later.

Now you have taken the time to determine what your property is. You should have a list of the different things that you own and their value listed next to them. Even if you do not have an exact amount, you still know the basic idea of your worth.

But that is not your worth just yet. You counted all your assets and now you need to get rid of the debt that you owe on this positive balance.

YOUR DEBTS: SUBTRACTING DEBT FROM PROPERTY

You need to take away the amount of money that you owe from the assets that you own. By doing this, you will be able to come to a true understanding of what your estate is worth. Just as we did with your property values, you now need to invest the time in determining what you owe. Here is a breakdown of all that you need to take into consideration.

Loans

The largest loan that most people have is their home. If you have a mortgage, a tax lien, or any other type of loan on your home, you will need to find out what the balance is. To determine the amount of money that you owe on your home, request a statement from your mortgage holder or your bank. This will provide you with several things, including the interest that you are being charged on the loan, which you will need later. You should know your monthly payment, the amount of years or payments you have left, and the total that you owe on the home mortgage (any and all that you have).

Do you have student loans? Do you have loans on your car? These all need to be considered in the same manner. Learn what the balance is, what your interest rate is, what you pay monthly, and the number of payments left until the debt is paid in full. If you have loans on any property, such as recreational vehicles, 401(k) loans, or debts that you owe to others, include them here in the same manner.

Credit Cards

The other costly debt that some people have is that of credit cards. Take time to go through all your credit card accounts and list what you owe on each one. Here, you should also write down the costs of the cards in interest, monthly payment amounts, as well as the total amount owed. This will help you to determine the amount that you owe.

With credit cards, the amount that you owe can go up and down quite a bit. It will ultimately be a factor about why you use the credit that you have. Determine the amount that you owe, realizing that this will change month by month depending on your credit usage.

Make sure to include all the charge accounts that you have which will include bank cards, credit lines through retailers, your home equity lines of credit, and any other debts that you have that allow you to charge your purchase. Some credit accounts do not have an actual credit card, but rather you will write checks for the amount you wish to draw out. Consider these in the same regard.

Your Future Debts

While you cannot know for sure what you will spend in the future, you can clearly see what the costs are in relation to some big expenses. For example, if you plan to pay for your child's education through college, you know that this will be a substantial debt. Your future debts can include any large expenses that you know are coming.

On that same token, you should take into consideration the amount of money you will be saving down the road, too. For example, if you have only a handful of payments left until your home is paid in full, you should consider this debt just as you would any other. But you should realize that you will have to readjust this amount within that time period as a positive balance account.

Do the Math

Now that you have it all figured out on paper, you can easily do the math and come up with the best plan for you.

Take the amount of real property value that you have and subtract from it the cost of your debt. By totaling all these beforehand, you know clearly what your property value and your debts are, and you can subtract the debts and see what you are worth.

Are you scared of that number? Are you worried that it is not enough? For some, it may even be a negative balance. Instead of worrying about this right now, you still should realize that you need to consider the value of these items as time goes by. For that, you need to consider the long-term look on your loan, as we will do in the next section.

WHAT DOES THE FUTURE HOLD IN WORTH?

You may think that you have a good net worth or perhaps not. But what you must realize is the fact that this number changes. If you go out and spend $1,000, that affects your net worth. If you pay off your vehicle, then your asset value rises and your debts fall. As you can see, managing your estate plan in terms of net worth is critical, and it is something you have to do on a regular basis. It will be necessary for you to track these changes yearly and readjust your estate plan to fit your current situation.

Not only does the financial aspect of your estate plan change quite a bit, but so does that of your life. Just think back ten years ago. What were you doing? Have you gotten married in that time? Perhaps you have had two children in the last ten years. You may have changed jobs, improved your income, purchased stocks, and so on. Each of these things plays a role in the outlook of your estate plan.

Should you have a large life change happen to you, you need to come back to your estate plan, especially your net worth, and make changes to it to reflect that information.

This can be especially important in situations such as getting married, getting divorced, and having children. The drastic changes that happen here are critical to your estate outlook. Changes affect not only your net worth but also the way that your estate is divided up among your family.

For many, they think they are giving their children what they deserve and even split things equally among them. Then, when you do die, you end up with one sibling getting more than the next. The problem with this is that the values of those stocks, those investments, and even the value of your home have changed. One child may get more than the next. Then what? You will have siblings that you thought you were providing equally to getting different amounts of assets and value.

As you can see, it is vitally important to come back to your assets and determine what they are worth now. This way, you get to leave your property and your assets to those that you want to have them, based on their value right now.

Now that you know your net worth, we can move into the dividing up of those assets to help protect your loved ones when you die. That process is called a will.

FACTORING IN SETTLEMENT COSTS

One of the key points to estate planning is planning for settlement costs, which is basically what we will provide you with throughout the rest of this book. Settlement costs are the costs to settle your estate that your heirs or those that are in your estate plan will have to do. These costs should be kept in mind along with your actual estate value.

Here are a few costs that should be considered and later planned for in your estate for settlement costs:

- The cost of your last illness, medical stay, or care for the last days or months of your life.

- The cost of your funeral, embalming, and burial.

- The cost of any debts that you have incurred that is not paid for at the time of your death.

- Probate administration expenses. These can include anything from court costs, to the preparation of final documents for court proceedings, and attorney fees.

- Death taxes or estate taxes, which you will learn much more about later on, are taxes that are levied on the value of your property.

The goal of estate planning is to plan for and minimize any and all of these costs as much as possible. Settlement costs can be enormous, especially when the value of your estate exceeds the estate tax threshold. Even for someone that has little in the way of value, settling an estate can be a very costly situation, costing most families thousands of dollars.

Yet you can plan for most of them, which is what the rest of this book reveals to you.

3

YOUR WILL: THE DEFINITION OF YOUR ESTATE PLAN

You have seen it on television shows. The family of a rich man is meeting, anticipating what they are being given in the will. They are eagerly sitting there, pretending to have cared about dear old Uncle John and telling stories about how much he touched their lives even though they have not seen him in at least four years. The meeting is about his will and what will be given to each of them for playing a role in his life.

Perhaps you cannot wait to be looking down on this moment when you finally get to reward those that you love with all that you have worked hard for. Perhaps you cannot wait to see those that have hurt you for so long crying when they realize that they were not included in your will. No matter what you are dreaming about, the will is an essential piece of legal work that should not be skipped.

It is so important that we have included it here, at the beginning of the estate plan. The will is what you say and command from your grave. It is your last will, your last way to make a mark on the world. No matter if you want your pet dog to have everything or if you want to give everything you worked hard for to charity, you have to define what you want to give, where to want it to go, and how you want your last wishes carried out.

The key to a will is to keep it up to date about you and your life. A will that is clearly defined and one that is current is the best piece of legal work that you have that can be used to honor your wishes. With the help of a will, you will be able to clearly define your loved ones' futures.

If you forget to go back to your will and include your newest grandchild or you forget to make changes to your child's college education requirements, they may end up losing out. If something changes down the road, include it in your will. You should come back to your estate plan, including your will, each year to consult it and consider any necessary changes that need to be made.

Even worse are the mistakes that can happen when it comes to making a will. If you do not include a skilled estate planning attorney in the development of your will, you will find yourself in even more hot water. The terminology and legal clauses that go into will planning can be quite difficult to understand, and they will confuse anyone that has not gotten his or her law degree.

The goal of a will is to define who will get what, but just an error in the wording of your will can put you in the position of not being able to get around taxes or it may include wording that can be contested, which means your heirs can fight the terms you set forth The end result is that a court of law defines your last wishes rather than you. It cannot be said enough that a quality estate planning attorney should be used to define your will.

One important definition that you need to take into consideration is that of a beneficiary. As you will see throughout this chapter, a beneficiary is an important person in terms of your loan. A beneficiary is the person that will profit from your will. For example, if you name your children as beneficiaries, they will get something from your will, as you define it. Heirs, businesses, and even charities can be beneficiaries in your will.

A will can be the sole piece of work that you do to protect your heirs. While an entire estate plan is the best route to go to fully care for your estate, you can simply have a will. There are several people that this can benefit. For example, if you are someone that is healthy and young, you may want to get certain things down in writing for "just in case" situations. For many, this means caring for their children in the event of a crisis.

Or, if you do need an estate plan and have not had the time to develop one just yet, a will allows you to buy some time until you get that estate plan done. If you are one to procrastinate, at least write your will because it will define exactly what you want to happen when you die, even though just having a will is likely to mean that your estate will end up in probate.

YOUR WILL IS A BACK-UP

In the estate planning process, a will can be a back-up piece of paper to your trust. There are a number of times when your will can help you to better define what you will be leaving and to whom you will leave it. Here are some times when having a will happens to be the better decision than having only a trust for your estate.

- Some property is better left in a will. For example, the car you own or the frequent flyer miles that you have are better off in a will than in a trust because it is too hard for these things to be managed through a trust. Most car insurance companies will not provide insurance to a car that is in a trust.

- If you happen to win the lottery and then you pass away, this extra and unexpected property is something you will want to give to those that you love, but who gets it? If you have not had the opportunity to get a change made to your estate plan, a will can be helpful. In this example, if you died just a few weeks after winning the lottery (would that not be your luck?), then the winnings of the lottery would be forwarded to the person named in your will as the residuary beneficiary. This person gets everything that is not specifically named in your will for someone else.

- A will is an absolute must for those that have minor children. Using a will to convey your named guardian for your children is the best vehicle to use. There simply is no other way to do this than in a will. You should also appoint someone in your will to manage the child's property and his or her money until he or she is old enough to manage these by himself or herself.

- Perhaps you want to disinherit someone in your estate because you do not want them to receive anything. The only way for you to do this is through a will. You can legally do this with a spouse or with a child. There are laws that govern this, though, that you need to know about.

- You will use your will to name your executor, too. We will discuss this a little later.

- If you know that you will own something in the future and want to make sure that it is divided the way that you want, then a will is a must. A will can include a clause that includes property that you believe is coming to you at some time in the future.

- You simply may not need anything else. In some states, if your worth is under a certain dollar amount, all that you need to make your wishes come true is a will. That is because the state does not require these situations to go into probate, which means what you want can be fulfilled.

As you can see, there are some things that a will can do for you that your general estate plan cannot do for you. You will want to invest the time necessary in getting this worked out with an attorney to ensure that your wishes come true.

GETTING YOUR WILL STARTED

As we have talked about, you need to have an estate planning professional, preferably an attorney, to handle the development of your will. This person should work closely with you to ensure that all your needs are met during the planning of the will. Once you have them selected, you can start planning your will.

First and foremost, you should find out your legal estate tax. You will learn more about this later, but for now just realize that it should be one of the first things that you talk about with your attorney. You need to know just how much money your estate will need to pay out in taxes when you die so that this amount is set aside for just that purpose and does not affect the items that you want to give to those that you are leaving behind.

The second step is to know your net worth and know what belongs to you and its value. So, who do you want to leave your money to? This is a personal decision and one that you should not make on your own but with your spouse and loved ones. Nevertheless, it is your money to do with what you see fit.

Take a moment to write down who you want to leave something to. Do you want to include all your children? Do you want your brothers, sisters, and your friend down the street to receive payments? You have to decide not only who gets your funds but also who you do not want to get a share. You may not want one of your children to receive any of your possessions.

For many, there is also a desire to provide your estate, or at least part of it, to charity. Perhaps you want the funds from your estate to go toward funding a new park in your neighborhood. If you do want such things to happen, then you need to decide this now.

At this point, you may not know what or how much you want to leave each of those that you love. Before you begin to figure that out, you should take some time to determine just what your options are, which means learning a bit more about wills. You will learn that here, of course, but for now, plan a meeting with your attorney to discuss who you want to include in your will and what the goals of your will are. The legalities of the will set up will depend on the goals that you have.

What Makes a Will Legal?

An important consideration is the legality of a will. No matter if you have every good intention, there are laws in place that can limit and even restrict what you are doing. There are some rules that make a will legal; in other words, if they are not fulfilled, then your will simply will not go through.

Here are some things that are required in order for your will to be considered a legal document:

- You have to be over the age of 18.

- You have to be of sound mind. Although this is continuously contested in the soap operas on television, it is not likely that this will be something contested in real life without real proof. Your attorney may go through a series of tests or they may have a doctor sign off on this if you are concerned that someone would contest your will on these grounds.

- Your will cannot be hand written but must be written on a typewriter or a computer.

- You must have two witnesses to sign your will. Your witnesses have to be over the age of 18, and they must be people that will not inherit anything in your will.

- You must have a date on the will of when it was created and signed.

- You must have an executor in your will.

- You must list at least one substantive provision. For example, you must leave your property to a named person in your will.

All these things will be required of your estate planning attorney to make sure of before he or she tells you that your will is ready to go.

Choosing Your Executor

The executor of your will is the person that will make sure that your wishes are carried out. There are many people that can be chosen for this job, but the best person to choose is the one that you trust the most. If you name a person as executor of your will, you trust them to make the right decisions about your hard earned money. You are giving them the ability to have those wishes carried out and also to consider any necessary work that goes along with the process.

When it comes to naming your executor, consider several things. First, you can have several people do the job. This does make things much more complicated, though, because they will all need to handle the responsibility and make decisions together. This may be a good idea, though, if you will be causing a family fight or conflict if you have just one person as your executor.

Once you have selected the right person for the job, you need to make sure it is okay with them. This should be an agreement that is made because the tasks of being an executor can be somewhat time consuming and quite a bit of responsibility. Do not be offended if the person you choose does not feel he or she is the right person for the job.

All wills legally require one executor to be appointed in them. One option that you have is to hire someone to execute your will that is not a "someone." Consider hiring a company or a bank to manage your estate after you die. While this technically sounds like a good thing, it does leave the personal touch off, which means decisions are based solely on getting the job done. That also means that they will likely charge fees for everything that they do for you.

The executor of your will is responsible for getting your probate taken care of, as well as supervising the property and funds transfers to those that you have deemed deserve it. He or she also has to take into consideration the estate tax that you may have to pay and file these payments. Your estate attorney should be able to help him or her through the process, but officially he or she needs to make decisions in this regard.

What Type of Will Is the Right Will?

You will be working with your estate planning attorney to create your will, but you should still realize the different types of wills and what they mean to you. You do have the option of using them, should they fit your need and you should, therefore, take them into consideration.

Simple Wills

A simple will is the most common type of will today. These wills are not joint wills, as they serve only for one person. In addition, they are a single piece of documentation that describes what your wishes are. When this type of will is used, it will name the document as your will. It will list who your beneficiaries are, including any charities that you are giving money to, and it will list their addresses and birth dates. In addition, it will name the executor of your will and possibly a secondary executor in case the first cannot provide for you. The will also will include the directions that you have for who will care for your children and your property, as well as distribute your assets as you deem.

Handwritten Wills

Although you can technically have a handwritten will, it is one of the most troublesome types of wills that you can have. If you do go this route, you will need to have the will written completely, including a date and signature of the person that the will is for. In addition, they are only recognized in a handful of states, so make sure that your state recognizes these wills. Handwritten wills are legally known as holographic wills.

The problem with these wills is that the judge in probate will worry that it is not the wishes of the person that wrote it but was forged. Some cases have been just like this. The handwritten will can also lead to a number of concerns about the proof that is required for the will to be considered legal. How will your heirs prove that you wrote it? Therefore, it is important to consider just how difficult it would be for you to type up a will and have witnesses watch you sign it.

Joint Wills

Another common type of will is the joint will. This type of will is one document that is used for the wishes of two people. Married people often consider a joint will believing that it is their only choice. This does not have to be the case, though. You can file two separate single wills when you are married. There is a real problem with this type of will, though.

Many judges will treat a joint will as a contract that cannot be contested even after you die. This is called a contractual will. That means that if your spouse dies before you do and the will says that all your money will go to taking care of your dog, then this cannot be changed by you later, even if your wishes change.

It should be considered a rare decision to select a joint will over other types of wills. Only go this route if your estate planning attorney says that it is the best thing for you, and then learn why that is the case. There are better solutions for you down the road, too.

Mutual Wills

Another type of will that you may be able to use is a mutual will. In this type of will, two people can have their wills or estate plans linked together — for example, if you and someone else have been working on a project for a long time and you want your assets or a portion of them to go to the project you have been working on. So, you can set up your will to include specialized amounts to be donated depending on who dies first. You can split money between several organizations this way so that no matter who dies first, the most important charity or organization gets those funds first. The legalities of this type of will are important to understand, though, so ensure that you work with an attorney that knows the ins and outs of mutual wills.

Statutory Wills

Statutory wills are a good idea that just does not work well. Only four states, Michigan, California, Maine, and Wisconsin, allow them. These wills come pre-made, and all you need to do is fill in the blanks and sign on the dotted line. While they seem like a good idea, there is one main problem with them. You cannot customize them. That means that even if you just want to put in one clause you cannot do so, and the end result is that you find yourself having to go with what is on the paper.

The only time when these wills are okay to use is when you plan to leave everything to your spouse, in which case there are no special instructions. Or, if your wife dies before or with you, you can add your minor child as the beneficiary to your estate.

Ethical Wills

If you have something to say to your loved ones, then an ethical will may be the way to go. Usually, an ethical will is one that is done separately from your legal will. It allows you the ability to talk about your thoughts, feelings, your concerns, and even your values. You can use it to tell stories about things that were important life altering situations or you can use it to help you share your thoughts on why you gave one person money and the next nothing.

Sometimes, people want to use ethical wills to make stipulations on their heir's ability to cash in on the estate. For example, you may put in your will that unless your grandson finishes college he does not get anything from your estate. While this can be something that you do, it becomes difficult to enforced. Even more so, someone has to take the time to understand what your goals are and to help make sure that the end result is achieved. You will also need to have a trust in place to manage these funds for the time being.

Other Types of Wills

Although the wills we have already mentioned are rarely used (except for the simple will) the following wills are additional options that you have that can be even more limiting. Most states have strict laws on these types of wills that you must know about before you attempt to use them.

- **Nuncupative:** This will, also known as an oral will, is one that is spoken. The only time that this will can be used, in most cases, is when someone is on their deathbed. If you are going to die within minutes, this type of will can be used in highly unusual circumstances.

- **Electronic Wills:** Another type of will that has been seen appearing is the electronic will. Only Nevada allows this type of will, though. If you have created your will in electronic format, such as on your computer, this could be an option, but it is not that easy. In addition to the actual electronic recording, you will also need some way of identifying that you wrote the will, which could include fingerprints, retinal scans, or even voice recognition. Sometimes it is required to have a specialized program to write the will that will include an electronic signature.

- **Video Wills:** You see these all the time on television, but no state allows a will to be video recorded as the sole way of communicating your wishes. You can recite your wishes over video and communicate your needs through video but only if you have a legal document in place beforehand. This is a good addition to your legal will, though, especially when you believe that the will will be contested.

Now that we have gone through a wide range of wills, you have to realize that the only fail safe type of will is a simple will. You should only use these other wills in extreme conditions in which they work for your special circumstances. Talk with your attorney to learn if one of them may be a better choice for your needs.

DEVELOPING A WILL

Now that you have a good understanding of what type of will you need, it is time to consider the legal inclusions in that will. What you must take into consideration is the need to have a will that is legally binding. Without the inclusion of some of the things and the right wording in your will, it can be contested either by your heirs or even by the judge in probate. That is what you want to avoid if you can.

Throughout the document, there are going to be different sections and terms used to help get your wishes represented clearly. With the right clauses, your wishes can be easily understood and clearly defined.

Clauses make up the important part of your will, and therefore, there are many of them. You need to know what these clauses are and what they mean. Lucky for us, it is easy to break them down and explain them.

Opening Clauses

The first type of clause is an opening clause. It provides the opening to your will, which includes your identification and any information that is necessary to move into the actual meat of the will. The opening clause also makes a statement about your "free will" in making the will and describes you as being "of sound mind." It also has to dictate that any will you may have written prior to this one is no longer valid.

In the opening clause, you will also identify those that are listed or included in some way in your will later on. Here, you simply introduce them as "my sister Betty," for example.

In addition, there is usually a tax clause entered into this part of your will. This clause will help to define what your tax strategy is and how you want those taxes to be paid on your estate. As we will talk about later, doing this is important to protecting your heirs, as well as protecting your estate. Adding the tax information here will help to deliver the information your heirs need from the start.

Giving Clauses

Now it is time to do the work of your will. The giving clause is the area of your will that comes after your opening clause and describes the meat of the will. Here, you get to name who is going to get your furniture, your home, and your other property. This part of the will is where you get to name your wishes, and for that reason you should consider it as being one of the most important parts of your will and even your estate plan.

The giving clause should be well worded. It should include all necessary information clearly presented without any assumptions. The good news is that you get to choose just how specific you want to be in the will. For some people, just being general about the gifts that they are giving is good enough. For others, it is important to be extremely detailed in each aspect of the will's gifts. Or you can use a combination of these things; for example, you may want to specifically include information about your high priced book collection, but you do not care as much about your furniture and clothing.

One route that you can go with your giving clause is to simply say that you would like all your property and your net worth to be divided among those that you name as beneficiaries equally. You may want to do this if you do not have specific needs and desires to divide your property among your loved ones. In this case, your net worth, whatever it is, will be divided equally among your heirs.

If you do not want an equal portion of your will to go to each of your heirs, then you need to be as precise and detailed as you can be about who is going to get what. Doing this will help to keep your wishes completely understood instead of allowing people to fight over each item that you own. It can also be important to do this if and when you have a large, extended family and want certain people to get better gifts than others or you want each person to get a specific item.

Now, there are three different types of giving clauses that you need to take into consideration for the types of giving that you plan to do. These clauses are in place to directly provide for your wishes.

- **Personal Property Clause:** The first of these is a personal property clause. Your personal property (as we have described in earlier sections) is both your tangible and your intangible property. In this part of the will, you need to include specific directions about what will happen to your personal items. This should include your valuable and sentimental property. In most cases, it will be important to you to list who gets the family heirlooms or other important items that you are leaving behind.

- **Real Property Clause:** Again, you know that your real property is the most valuable part of your estate. In this case, you will want to divide up the property among those that you want to own it. This clause identifies what your real property is and tells of your wishes about who will get that property or how it will be divided. In most cases, people are specific about this type of property simply because of the value that it has.

- **Residuary Clause:** The third part of your giving clause is that of the residuary clause. This type of clause is important, especially if you do not take the time to come back and make changes to your will as you should. It will determine exactly who gets whatever else you have not mentioned in your will. For example, if you write up your will today and include your son Max as the residuary beneficiary, then he would get anything that is not listed specifically in other areas of your will. If you purchase a boat in the next year and die without including something specific in your will about the boat, Max would inherit the boat because of this power. This clause is essential simply because if the will is not updated or you forget to mention something, it is a catch all for the rest of your belongings.

As a side note, there are additional clauses in your giving clause that help to define exactly who will manage your estate and what powers they will have. These clauses are called the appointment clause and the fiduciary powers clause. There are additional clauses as well which have little to do with the actual estate you are planning to take care of. Instead, they may be legal terminology that just has to be there but does not affect the way that you hand out your estate.

Ending Clause

Now that you have your wishes spelled out in the giving clauses, you can then end your will. You have given away your property and you have specifically described everything that you want to happen when you die. Now, it is time to sign on the dotted line. The ending clause provides for the signature (in its own separate clause called the signature clause, of course) In addition, your witnesses will need to sign your will at this point. The date will also need to be placed in this clause.

When you sign your will, you state that you are doing so by your own free will and of sound mind. When your witnesses sign your will, they are attesting to the fact that you are not being forced to sign it in any way and that they are witnessing the action. Your witnesses cannot be someone that you list as a beneficiary in your will. These people need to be people that do not benefit from your will in any way.

Now, there is the matter of probate to consider. You can avoid the need to provide witnesses during probate if you select and have your witnesses sign correctly. This is called having the will "self proved." To do this you will need to have the witnesses' signatures done in a specific way. First, they will need to have their signatures acknowledged as well as being witnesses. You also need them to provide affidavits stating that they saw this happen and signed your will. When this is done, probate will not require that your witnesses come forward stating that they saw you sign your will.

That is it. That is what goes into the will. While you understand this, you realize that the process of determining who will get what can be more challenging and ultimately will take you the most time. Yet it is fundamentally necessary to go through each of your needs carefully so that you do not forget something that can cost you dearly, or rather, cost your loved ones dearly.

WHAT CANNOT GO IN A WILL

This book describes the process of developing an estate plan, which is much more than just managing your will. In an estate plan, you will work to develop a plan for everything that you own and wish to happen when you die. But a will is an excellent part of that estate plan because it can define much of what you are looking to have spelled out. Although a will can do quite a bit for your estate plan, it cannot do everything.

There are a number of things that cannot be included in your will. Your estate plan will cover most of these, though, through other means, but you still need to know what you cannot put in your will.

If you list any of your property in another part of your estate planning or place other ownership on the property, then it cannot be included in your will. If it is included there, the ownership remains dependant on the other form instead of on the directions you provide in your will. Your attorney will tell you specifically what can and cannot be included for your special circumstances, but here is a general list of property that, if placed in other parts of your estate plan, cannot be placed in your will.

- **A living trust**: A living trust is something we will talk about later, but for this purpose anything that you put into a living trust will be executed to those individuals as the trust deems, not your will.

- **Life insurance**: If you have a life insurance plan set up that is payable to a beneficiary, the funds must go to that beneficiary, not to those listed in your will.

- **Joint tenancy property**: If you die and leave a spouse behind, the share that is yours goes to them. If you are the last to die, then you can put this property into your will.

- **Pay on death accounts:** If you set up an account that pays out when you die, then the person named to receive those funds in the account paperwork will get them, not the person you name in your will.

- **Other accounts:** If you have retirement accounts, 401(k)s, or other accounts like this that have funds in them at the time of your death, those funds go to the person or people named as your beneficiary, not to those that you name in the will.

Now, what does this information mean to you? If you do not want the person that is listed as your beneficiary on these types of accounts to get your funds, then you need to take into consideration changes to them. Talk to your life insurance provider and get this changed. Contact the holders of your other accounts and fix this problem now because your will cannot do it for you.

ADDITIONAL WILL CONTENTS AND CONCERNS

The process of making a will is a bit more complicated than what is seems here. In the next chapter, we will talk about the legal aspects of the will, including some important aspects. But there are a few parts of the will that we have not talked about that should be mentioned here. Take into consideration these aspects of the will's make-up as well. You may find it necessary to add these things into your will.

Explanations: Feel the Need?

If you feel that it is important to tell those that you love why you did what you did in your will, then you should do just that. Leaving explanatory letters that will accompany your will is a good idea, especially for those that face worries about what their heirs will think.

To get this letter started, you will first start with an explanation of what the letter is. It will help to clarify what you want done with the letter, as well as help those that are handling your death understand what it is. There is no real legality to these types of letters, but they can be somewhat confusing if the person does not know full well what they are getting into. The fact is that having this letter done can help you to feel better about the decisions that you make in your will.

Why should you write this type of letter? You do not have to, but if you have feelings, thoughts, or expressions that you would like to make, this letter is a good place to do so. You may want to explain to your family and friends why you left the money, property, or other items in your will to those that you did. This is a good way to talk about why it was important to you to give that old piece of art to your daughter and why you wanted to give your son money.

Although legally you do not have to do this, it can be helpful to talk about what you are giving your loved ones when you die before you die. You should sit down and talk about why one is getting more than another and why you feel it is much more important that someone get something rather than another. Even if you do this (or if you do not) you may want to define why you did not give out your property evenly to all your heirs. No matter if you make the decision to leave your property unevenly distributed because you have already given out a large amount of your money to one person and not to another or because you feel someone has a greater need, you may want to clarify this now in a letter.

Another reason to leave this type of letter is to talk about your feelings. Perhaps you want to explain why you are leaving all your money to your favorite charity. Perhaps you want to tell someone what they have meant to you during your lifetime. You may want to communicate a number of gratitude and sentiments to those that you are leaving behind. There does not have to be any types of corollary to this and what you leave in your will, though.

One thing that people are tempted to do is to leave bad sentiments and feelings to those that they may not have liked all that much. It can be helpful to do this when you feel the need, but you may want to consider not doing so. Legally speaking, there is no reason why you cannot do so. But you may want to save those sentiments for a less public manner.

Finally, this letter is also a tool to help you express your needs and desires for those that you leave behind, from children to pets. You can easily remark on these subjects here so that those that are caring for these important parts of your life do so with the best of wishes and trust. Again, nothing here is legally binding, but it can be the perfect place to state your wishes in these regards.

Pets and Wills

If you love your pet and want to make sure that they are well taken care of when you pass away, then you can include information regarding your pet in your will. There are a number of things that you can do, but there are also considerations that must be made about what you cannot do. Beyond anything else, you cannot leave money or property to your pet directly. What you can do, though, is to provide for your pet through other methods.

Your pet is considered property, not a beneficiary. That means that you will need to set up care for your pet. If you attempt to leave property or a trust for your pet, it will likely be given to your residuary beneficiary and not to the pet.

One of the best moves to make in taking care of your pet is to do so with the help of a friend. Determine what would happen to your pet if you died. Who would care for it? That person can be named in your will as the beneficiary who will get your pet when you pass away. You can also give them some amount of money that is to be used for the care of the pet. Doing this is one of the best routes you can take because it provides the care that is necessary for your pet.

There are some states that allow a trust to be set up for the pet's care. If your state is one of these, you will need to set up a trust (which we will talk more about later) that will define what your goals, needs, and requirements are. The trust can be used to care for a pet only in states in which this is recognized. Your attorney can help you to determine if this is a possibility where you live.

Who Will Fight My Will? Will They Win?

With the drama of television and movies, many are afraid that the will that they put so much thought and heart into, that has their wishes and their needs, may somehow be contested and will end up meaning nothing. Although this worry is there for a good reason, because you can have your will contested, it is rare that anyone will win this type of legal proceeding.

The only things that can make your will null and void are the things we have talked about. If you are over the age of 18, have made the will without any coercion or under duress, and are mentally fit, then there is little hope that your will can be successfully contested. It is quite difficult to prove these allegations, too. The burden of proof is on the person that is claiming it, not on the court. A court will not say that a person is incapable of making their own decisions unless they are far out of it. In addition, unless there is proof of something being very wrong, it is highly unlikely that the will can be changed.

Even still, you may be concerned. The good news is that your lawyer can help make your will stronger so that it will not be contested. He or she may recommend certain legal filings that will provide additional protection to you. If you are unable to sign your name or have other conditions in which you cannot communicate, a good attorney will be more than willing to help you, and in some cases, can write your name for you. An attorney can also testify for you on grounds that he or she knew your competence at the time of the will signing. Meet with and consider talking to someone about this as soon as possible, especially if there is a large amount of property that is in question.

Keep Your Will Safe

Now that your will is written, you need to keep it safe. Where should you put it? What should you do to it? There is much debate about this. Some attorneys feel strongly about this decision and it makes good sense to follow what they say.

First, the original will is the most important piece of paper. This has the actual signatures on it that make it authentic. This piece of paper should be kept secured and carefully protected.

- If you want to keep it in your home, only do so if you can provide it with a fire-proof safe. Unless you can ensure that the will can be kept safe from any possible damage, then do not keep it at home.

- If you want to keep it with your attorney, you can do that also. He or she should be able to provide you with a safe at his or her office. He or she can also be left with instructions on what to do when you die so as to not involve anyone else in the decision.

- If you want to keep your will in a safety deposit box, you can do this, too. But a word of caution here: If you live in a state in which the contents of a safety deposit box will be sealed on your death until probate, then you do not want to keep your will there. That is because it will not be accessible until that time, making all your work that much less important. Instead, use one of the other areas to store your will. If you live in a state that does not seal safety deposit boxes, then you can use these locations.

You should appoint someone as your personal representative and executor. He or she should receive a copy of your will. Only your attorney should make these copies for you, though. Some people also like to give a copy of their will to several people, namely those that are listed in your will. This is fine, too, because it helps them to make plans for your death in advance, so there are no surprises for them later.

Finally, you should have an unsigned copy of your will with you at home. You will need to come back to your will several times to ensure that it is still up to date and accurate in the information that it provides to you. This means that you will want to have a copy that you can reference. This copy can be used to take notes on, if you want to talk to your attorney about them.

You do not have to tell anyone that you have signed your will. You do not have to tell anyone where your will is, except for your executor. But it is always best to leave the surprises out of your will.

Keep Them Out!

Are there people that you plan to keep out of your will? If so, then you need to make sure to put them into your will. The problem with leaving people out of your will altogether is that they may feel insulted so much so that they may challenge your will. Instead, just list them in your will as receiving nothing. Your attorney will be able to use the correct language for this situation.

You can also leave them something small so that they are included in the will but only by a fraction. By doing this it will also serve to protect you from those family members that seem to think they deserve something from your estate.

MONITORING YOUR WILL THROUGHOUT YOUR LIFE

You have heard the saying that life just happens. With a will you need to make sure that when life happens, your will reflects what has happened to you. People get married, divorced, have kids, sell it all, invest it all, and even lose it all. As you go through your life, monitor what your will reflects to ensure that it provides for what you do want to happen when you are no longer alive.

The most important times to reassess your will include the times when your family make up changes. For example, if you get married, everything changes to include your spouse. If you have a new child, you want to include them in your will as well. If you have a divorce, you want to go back and change the funds and property that you are giving your soon to be ex-wife or ex-husband. You will also want to look at your will for other reasons, too.

For example, if one of your heirs dies, then you will want to remove them from your will and redirect their inheritance. Even more important is to reassess your will if your spouse dies. Most people leave most or all their belongings to their spouse, and if they pass away, you need to take this time to update your will to reflect the new need.

There may be events that happen in your life to make you change the way that you feel about those in your will. If you are considering a change because you want to pull someone out of your will, make sure that you are making the right decision. Take the time to seriously think about this decision. Of course there are other reasons you may need to change your will, such as losing a large amount of money or winning the lottery.

Need to Make a Change?

If you do need to make a change to your will, the process is not that difficult. That means there is no excuse not to get this done.

There are two different methods to making this happen. The most straightforward way of changing your will is to completely rewrite it. Do not worry, since you are likely only making a few changes to the contents of the will. It is a matter of going into a file, making the changes, and printing a new document. Your attorney will have this information on file for you, so the process can literally take one meeting.

If you do not want to do this to your will and just want to make some changes to it, then you can have your attorney draw up a codicil. This is a document that will accompany your will that makes changes. You should not attempt to write this document yourself because it must specifically reference portions of your will in legal format. Your attorney will need to prepare this document for you so that it will be legally binding.

You should go the route of a codicil if and when you want to only make minor changes or when your competency at the time of executing the codicil may be challenged in some way.

YOUR WILL'S STATUS

You have done your part. You have written your will. You feel good about it and know that those that you love the most will be well taken care of. That is it; you are done, right?

All you can do is keep your will up to date and to make sure that it is legally sound. But you may be wondering what happens when you die. Now, we will dedicate a whole chapter to the wonderful world of probate, but before we do that, we want you to realize the process of your will's status.

There are three phases of your will's status. During this time, your will is being considered. Is this real? Is this what he or she wanted? Should what is written here be honored?

The status of your will when you die will fall into one of these:

Testacy: This is where you want to be. In this status, your will is valid and it has all it needs to be held up in court. If you die testate, that means that your will is valid in that your wishes are clearly defined throughout the document. Your wishes can be carried out and you will die knowing that it is in good hands.

Intestacy: If you die without a valid will, you die in intestate, which means that the legal system gets control of your estate and will determine who gets what. The laws of intestate succession are used to determine what happens to your estate. Laws in each state are somewhat different but their basic standpoint is the same. They will take your estate and divide it among those that are considered to be your heirs. If you want funds to go to someone else that is not a relative of yours, then they are out of luck. Even worse, if you do not have any living relatives, the end result is that the state ends up with your estate.

Partial Intestacy: Here, you are someplace in the middle. You have a will but there is something wrong with it. For some reason, it may not be legally binding or there may be something that is left out of it. For example, if you do not include a residuary clause in your will, and you forgot to include something, there is no one to pass it on to. When you are in partial intestacy, once again the state gets to decide who gets your property by using these laws. The best way to avoid this is to ensure that your attorney has made certain each part of your will is binding and that the will is complete. This is another reason to hire a professional to handle your estate planning.

Planning your will is not nearly done. There are going to be other things that you need to know along the way. For that, the next chapter is written.

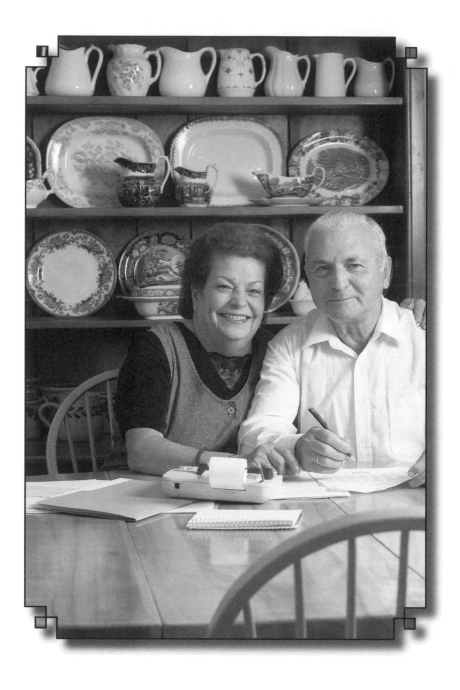

LAWS THAT YOU HAVE TO DEAL WITH

Although will planning is about making peace with your property and doing whatever you want with it, the fact is that there are also laws that must be followed. Sometimes, these laws can limit what you can do. Each one is set up with some benefit, of course, yet it is important for you to take into consideration how each one affects you.

Working with your attorney will help you to overcome some of the obstacles that you face in will planning. It is essential that you understand that some things are not as easy to plan as others are. Due to this, we have included the following information.

Each state has their own set of laws regarding wills. These laws affect not only what you can do in your will but also how your estate plan will be carried out after you are gone. Understanding these laws can help you safeguard yourself, your property, and your heirs. Most of the time, setting up your property in a will can be enough to circumvent these laws so that they work in your favor.

One important thing to realize is where these laws are coming from. They are coming from, not the federal government, but your state government.

Each state has their own set of unique laws governing wills. Therefore, the information that we include in this section of the book is not going to be 100 percent accurate for each person because each state has a unique way of protecting its citizens. This is yet another reason that you need to have the help of an estate planning attorney at your side during the process. You need him or her to help decipher the laws of your state and protect you with those laws.

Not all the statutes and laws that are in place are bad things. Most of them are quite helpful in protecting you and your heirs, especially if things change from what your will says. They also help to define specific elements, should it not properly be covered in your will. For example, it is essential for certain payments, like that of the death tax, to be paid, but who will pay it? These statutes help to answer those questions so that there is no question upon death.

As you prepare your will, pay attention to these statutes and laws. You should have talked to your attorney about them and know full well how they affect your will and estate plan. Planning around and with them can make a difference in helping to protect you from the start.

ABATEMENT STATUTES AND LAWS

The most common of the various laws that will affect the outcome of your will is the abatement statutes. In simple terms, an abatement statute is in place to help figure out what to do when your estate is not worth what your will says it should be. Who will get what, now that there is not enough to give? You may think this is not going to be a problem, but it happens more than you may think. Costs, life emergencies, doctor's bills, or just unplanned for expenses are in place often after a person passes on and they may not be accounted for in the will.

There is also the problem that arises when people plan to have money to leave behind but end up with debts that need to be paid instead. Abatement statutes help to define what should happen when you die and leave behind debt.

The definition of an abatement statute is simple: It is the process of reducing or lessening something so that all parties can be equally paid as they should be. These laws do change from state to state, yet they all have one goal: to help determine who should get the necessary funds and how debts should be paid down.

Abatement statutes also define what happens in your estate first. For most cases, debts must be paid down within a certain time frame before the actual value of the estate can be shared between your family members. The fact is that breaking down these numbers and the order in which they will be paid is crucially important. Sometimes, if you have residue in your estate plan, which means that there are extra funds in it, these funds may "abate" before the funds that are set aside to pay to your heirs as you have decided.

So, what can you do about these laws? First, you should know what they are. Work with your attorney specifically on this topic so that you can fully understanding what is likely to happen should there be a need for an abatement statute to occur.

Then, plan for it. You can put language into your will that can help make your wishes known, as far as who should pay what. Most of the time, your attorney will be able to provide for specifics on how your assets will be used to pay off debt, for example. You can also specify in what order your estate should be used to do this. Therefore, you still do have some say in how your money is used to pay down your debts and how abatements affect your estate.

While this can seem confusing, it does not have to be. With the right language in your will, it can easily be spelled out. For example, if you want to leave your children an equal share of your estate, then you do not want to spell out exact dollars in your will. Instead, using language that says "equal parts" will help to work around abatements. If your estate was valued at $500,000 and you said in your estate plan that you wanted each of your five children to receive $100,000, this could be a potential problem. If your investments do not do as well as you think they will, there may be only $400,000 in your estate. Then, with this type of language, there is a problem, and abatement laws must be used to determine who gets what.

This same process can be used to help define what happens to debts that you owe. When the debts, such as medical expenses, credit card debt, or other debts, are paid, with the correct language in your will, your heirs still get to receive what you want them to.

Your will may not be worth what you had planned for in dollars and cents, but with the right language, your wishes can play out. After your debt is paid down, then you can distribute your funds and estate to your heirs the way that you want to. Unfortunately, it is difficult to do this in numbers, but in percentages it works well. For example, you can have your spouse get 50 percent of the remaining estate, while each of your two children will get 25 percent. This way, you still determine the amounts that work for your wishes, but safeguard against abatements.

It Is Not Their Debt

One common misconception is that when you die your debts go with you. That is not the case, and there are going to be people, usually your heirs, that have to pay off what you owe. This is normally done through your estate. We will learn more about this in the chapter about probate; for now, you need to fully understand that you have to plan for debts that you may owe when you die. No matter how well you plan and how much you are valued at, you still need to take this into consideration or someone else will have to deal with it.

This book has talked about how to plan for debts in your estate plan by realizing that you must factor them into determining the value of your estate. If you do not do this, you cannot have an accurate estimate of your estate's value. Even those that have good intentions of paying down all their debt need to figure it in, because, in the worst case scenario, if you die tomorrow, it is there to be dealt with.

Abatement Happens

Even with good planning, some wills and estates will enter into abatement. When abatement does happen in the case of a will or estate, the state's statutes will determine where money will go. If you have debts that need to be paid down, then the order in which they will be paid and the money that will be used to pay them is determined by those statutes. It may come from the bottom of your will, so the funds you set aside to some long lost friend may be used. Or your heirs may become responsible for it. The end result, though, is that your estate will pay off this debt.

If you do not include the right clauses and language in your will to put aside an abatement and it happens because your will does not have the right amount in it to provide to your heirs as your will states, then abatement statutes will determine how the funds will be paid and in what order your estate will be divided.

Your state may have a UPC, or Uniform Probate Code, which helps to determine this. Ask your attorney what your state's laws are and what will happen if your estate enters into abatement.

ANTILAPSE STATUTES

Another problem that must be handled is that of antilapse. Should someone in your will pass away before you do, there has to be some law in place to help determine what to do with their share of your estate.

There are laws in place to fix this problem, as best that it can be, but it is also up to you to protect yourself against this type of situation.

If you do not make plans about how to handle this situation, then these statutes are in place to make those decisions. Yet you can circumvent those problems by naming a contingent beneficiary to your will. This person will be the catch all for your estate. For example, you may leave your cousin James $20,000. But if he does not survive you, then where will those funds go? If you have named your son as your contingent beneficiary, he would receive those funds.

Some states have antilapse laws while others do not. If you want to specifically say what happens to your estate should someone in your will pass away before you, get it written into your will through a contingent beneficiary. But this may not be necessary if you live in a state in which there is not one of these statutes. In this case, your property would be part of your in limbo property or property that does not have someone to claim it. In this case, it would fall to your residuary clause, which names those that would receive this type of property. This person will get anything that is not specifically named in your will.

ADEMPTION STATUTES

Yet another consideration is that of ademption. In ademption, there are laws in place which protect heirs that do not or cannot receive what you leave to them. If you, for some reason, include property in your will and estate to someone and that property is no longer part of your estate, then there are laws that play a role in this situation.

For example, let us say that you leave your set of fine china to your daughter. But if you have sold the set prior to passing away to help pay down your medical debt, then that is no longer a piece of property that can be passed on to your daughter. The ademption clause and statutes will come into play in this case.

These laws vary from state to state, but ademption is something to consider planning for. Your heir may be able to claim the property if he or she can prove that you were not competent at the time the property was sold or given away. If and when this happens, your heir may have some ability to get those pieces of property, but this is hard to prove and difficult to make happen.

Another time when the ademption statutes come into play is when you have given your daughter that china already. While this is not a problem, assuming that the correct gift taxes are used, it still will be property that is considered in ademption because it is no longer part of your estate when you die. Any property that is not part of your estate when you die is considered to be adeemed or unable to be divided. This also is the case for property which somehow ends up missing.

If you include property in your will that is considered to be adeemed property, the ademption clause will be used to help determine what should happen, if anything can be done. It also helps to determine if your heir should receive anything in the will. In addition, the statutes will say what that beneficiary can receive.

You should plan for this type of scenario with your attorney. Your attorney can help you determine the "what ifs" that are important in determining where your property will go. There can be additional language in your will to help protect you from this type of scenario, as well as what can remedy what will happen if you have property that cannot be included in your will because you are not in ownership of it any longer.

DEATH AND DIVORCE: TWO COMMON CONSIDERATIONS

Although no one wants to believe that it could happen, it can happen. If you find yourself filing for divorce some time in the future, you may not change your will before you pass away, for whatever reason. You are thinking to yourself that there is no way that you will get divorced. Your marriage is solid, and there is nothing to worry about. The statistics, though, show something different. The fact is that divorce happens to one out of every two marriages — 50 percent of the time. You need to plan for it.

The other situation that most people do not want to think about is that of your spouse dying before you do. In cases like this, there is no way to foretell what is going to happen. The fact is that a freak accident can happen tomorrow and whatever your will says is what happens.

Of course, as we are talking about the laws governing wills it is important to realize that if you do not plan for one of these events and they end up happening, you will find your will is left open to what these laws dictate. Therefore, it is important to work closely with your attorney to determine what you can do and what you should do to protect yourself from these situations.

Divorce: Planning for It

Even if you feel that there is a 100 percent chance that your marriage will be successful, you still need to use your will to protect your other heirs from a potential divorce. If you do not plan for it in your will, you may not change your will right after filing, and this can leave a possible problem should something happen to you.

Many people that do file for divorce do not make changes to their will right away or they simply keep putting it off. When this happens, the risks are inevitable. Sometimes people do not want to make changes in their will because doing so would ultimately say that they are admitting that their marriage is over. Or you may just forget to do so or keep putting it off. In any case, not making changes can lead to mistakes.

Yet that is not always the case. Many of the states today have taken into account divorce since it plays such a large role in people's lives. If and when there is a divorce that has not been changed in the will, there is still some protection for those that are left behind.

In some states, if your divorce is final and your ex-spouse is still named in your will, that spouse will not be allowed any of what you have left to them even if you do not make these changes before you die. In most cases, your estate is protected from claims that are filed against your estate by your ex-spouse. This means that they are not allowed to claim even what the will says is for them.

Yet it is also important to note that, if you want your spouse to get some of your estate after you are gone, this should be specifically included as a divorced spouse. If the right language is not used, there could possibly be a problem with the claim.

Even still, this is only the case in some states, not in all, and therefore, you should not assume that your estate is protected from your spouse unless you specifically make it so in your will. You should make sure that you do not rely on what the statutes are to handle situations like this. You should plan for this to happen so that your beneficiaries are the people that you want to receive your estate.

Death at the Same Time

Sometimes, death happens to both of you at the very same time, which can pose a real problem in will planning. Let us say that you both die in the same fatal car accident. Unfortunately, doctors cannot determine who died first, and therefore, the will that you have designed for situations in which one of you dies before the other cannot be used. The end result is that you have to rely on the state's statutes regarding this type of situation to determine what happens to your will and your estate.

All states have some form of law that offers protection and understanding in situations like this. These laws are called Uniform Simultaneous Death Act. This law is important to understand when there is a need to determine who died first. If your will has specific language in it that talks about surviving your spouse (which most wills will include if you are married), then this is an important statute to understand.

In most cases where there cannot be any assumption of who has died first in a simultaneous death, it is determined by these laws that you both survived the other. Each will and estate plan is executed assuming that you survived your spouse. That way, your property is divided the way in which your will determines if you were to live longer than your spouse did.

In most cases, this is good news because it allows your estate to avoid going through probate twice. In addition, it can save you money in estate costs. Yet if these are not your wishes, then it becomes a problem that you need to address beforehand. To protect yourself from such problems, you should include a survival clause in your will. This will make the necessary provisions for this type of situation based on the best and most profitable method according to what you and your attorney determine.

This is important in cases when you do not die at the same time but within a short time of one another. If one spouse is injured and dies days after the other, the possible problem here is that the estate will end up passing through estate probate twice because the first to die will have their will go into effect, giving the other their estate. When you use a survival clause, you are able to side step this process. Should the person that receives your estate die within a certain amount of time after you do, you will void that part of your will and the estate will pass to the other beneficiaries that you have determined. This keeps your estate out of probate for at least one round. You can add language into your will that says that the beneficiary must survive 30, 60, or some other number of days after you to receive your will's specifications.

Each of these situations shows you how you will need to handle the planning of your estate in cases where laws are in place that can alter what your wishes happen to be. It is important to make these changes in your will so that you can avoid possible problems later.

Not all laws and statutes can be changed by your will as we have shown you. There are a handful of laws that you will have to deal with when creating your will that cannot be sidestepped or overcome easily.

SOMETIMES LAWS GET IN THE WAY NO MATTER WHAT

Sometimes, there are laws that states have on the books that you just cannot overlook or somehow get around. These laws are part of the building process of a will, something you need to learn about. Even if you do not like what you see, it is what the law dictates and, in most cases, even if you include language in your estate that says that you do not want this to happen, it still may.

Here, we will go through some of the various laws that could affect the outcome of your will and estate. Each state has different laws that need to be taken into consideration.

In some cases, these laws are in place to protect your heirs if you are being malicious or otherwise causing them financial harm by trying to leave them nothing in your will. The state will then determine if the will should be honored and otherwise provide for your heirs. The fact is that many people try to include such things in their will and spend thousands of dollars trying to make it happen only to find out that probate changes everything anyway. Therefore, understanding these laws will save you time and money in the long run. If you do not want your will to be voided, you need to understand these statutes and laws fully.

Community Property Stipulations

There are some laws that protect community property, or property that is shared between you and your spouse. But it is not just your home that is being referred to here like many people think. The fact is that any money made or anything in ownership or acquired during your community property state of living is divided equally between the spouses. Therefore, if you die while living in a community property state, at least 50 percent of what you own will be left to your spouse because it is their property as well.

Not all states have this — only a handful do. These include:

- Arizona

- California

- Idaho

- Louisiana

- Nevada

- New Mexico

- Texas

- Washington

- Wisconsin (Marital property instead of community property)

In these states, you are required to leave your spouse 50 percent of what you own, and that includes anything that has been purchased or acquired in virtually any legal way during your marriage. The only type of property that you can completely call your own is any gift or inheritance that was received by you personally and solely. The only other property that may qualify is property that you owned prior to getting married (and you can show that you have owned it for that amount of time). Yet even this is subject to determination by probate.

If your sole property becomes community property, which is something that can happen if you place funds or other property with what you both own, then it can be considered the same as community property. Therefore, if you have this type of property and you do not want to it fall under this realm, keep it separate in some way.

Those states that do not have this law often have other laws that dictate how much of your estate is yours.

Common Law States

The other states all have what is called common law in regards to property ownership in a marriage. In these states you do still have to divide the property between the two of you, but it is not necessarily an equal share as it is in a community property state. This is determined through the spousal elective shares law that the state has in place in which your spouse can say that he or she has a claim to some of your property. The amount of your estate that your spouse can claim is determined by these laws. Each state offers a different determination on what that is, though. Work with your attorney to determine this.

If you have wishes as far as where your property goes and want to provide for that in your will, you can, but that does not mean it has to be honored. It is up to your spouse to determine what he or she wants. If you provide for more than what the state's elective share does, then your spouse can accept that amount. But if you try to provide them with less than this amount, then your spouse does not have to accept that amount but can go for the higher amount as defined by law.

In doing this, there are many problems. Your estate value is then going to be totally off. Again, when your estate's value changes your estate must be handled by law in determining who gets what and where it all goes. For this reason, you should never try to leave your spouse less than what your state's elective shares law requires or you may have less say in what happens to your money.

Each state has its own amount that is considered to the proper amount that should be provided. Elective shares can range from as low as three percent of your estate up to fifty percent of the estate. In some states, this amount is determined by how long you were married with increasing value the longer you are married. In other states, there are set amounts that determine it; for example, it may be 40 percent no matter how long you have been married.

You cannot side step these measures. For example, if you try to by moving property around before you die so that your spouse cannot include it in the value of the estate, this can be something that is placed back into the value of the estate should it be deemed possible. These laws are in place to protect the surviving spouse from your efforts to limit what they can claim as their own.

Let us say that you know you are dying and therefore move your property into your son's name. You are hoping that your property does not fall claim to your spouse's rights to that property. You have transferred it, so why would it? If you die within a certain amount of time after doing this type of transfer, the value of that property transfer can be added back into your estate and your beneficiaries cannot claim it. This is called an augmented estate.

If there are problems in your marriage and you do not want to leave your spouse anything, you should consider filing for divorce, which can provide you with more protection. Although you may not realize it, all your hard work in keeping your spouse from getting your property may just fly right out the door when the state takes a look at what you are doing. And, believe us, they will. Try to handle anything like this before you die so that you do not leave your estate and beneficiaries in the hole later.

Protecting Your Homestead through Your Will

There are a handful of states that provide a homestead law which allows you to help protect your family by maintaining your homestead, including your home and some property that is around it. The will is set up to help maintain this property and therefore is an excellent consideration, especially when you have quite a bit of land. If you have minor children, this may also be an ideal way to make sure they have a home for some time after your death.

If you wish to use this type of tool to help protect your family, you should pay close attention to how you will make that happen. Work with your attorney to include a homestead protection in your will if your state allows for it.

As part of this protection, you should also consider the homestead exemption laws that are in place in some states. This is a tool that you should consider if you fear that your spouse and/or children may be forced to pay a considerable amount of debt after you die. If you owe money and have this stipulation in your will, it helps to protect the home from being taken to pay the debt. But it is not a sure thing.

This type of law helps give your family some time to find ways to pay the debt, perhaps by selling something. By doing this, it helps keep creditors from kicking the family to the curb. It does not mean, though, that creditors cannot force the sale of a home because if not enough money can be found, this may be necessary. Nevertheless, it buys them some time.

One thing that you should do is find out if your state has any type of exempt property clauses. While most of your intangible personal property, such as your cash, cannot be kept away from creditors that have valid claims against you, sometimes your tangible property can be. That means that you can find value in a protective clause that allows your family to keep some of this type of property. Your attorney can help you determine if your state does offer this and what you can do to protect it.

Family Allowance Laws Protect Your Family

There are many problems that happen to families when the main financial provider dies. If you are the one that your family relies on to pay the bills, you may believe that your family can use whatever you have given them to keep on paying the bills and doing what they need to in order to keep themselves safe if you die. Yet what you may not realize is that probate takes a long time to go through. Until it does, your family may be without anything from you.

First, you do want to plan for situations in which your family will receive as much support as possible should you die. We are not saying not to plan for this, as that is what estate planning should do. But what you do need to consider is when those funds will be available to your family.

If you wish to make sure your family is protected upon your death, do not just include your wishes in a will. Instead, you need to make sure that your family is given what is called a family allowance until probate can be settled. It can take a year or more for that to happen in some states. If a mortgage payment is missed for just two or three months (usually just two), they are already risk losing their home.

A family allowance is just what it sounds like, and it is a near immediate tool that you have available to you. If your estate enters probate without this type of statute in place in your will, your family cannot tap into the funds that you have allocated to them until all your debts have been paid in full, which can take some time to make happen. A family allowance, though, can be paid out during this time to help keep the family living in the same manner that they need to.

But how much they get is another story. You see, there is an important consideration that each estate must go through. The determination of how much your family can receive is determined by how much your family's expenses are, as well as what your estate's value is. This determination is based on the state's statutes for it. Some states allow for more to be used. There is no doubt that your family will need to determine what is needed and show proof that it is needed in order to remain living the life they are used to living.

You should closely work with your attorney to determine what this allowance is likely to be. An estate planning attorney will be able to help you determine what it is so that they can help you to plan for just how much your family will receive. If you do not feel that it will be enough and your family will need additional income to make it through this time, you will want to set up a separate gift giving strategy that will provide funds to your beneficiaries. This can be a valuable tool for protecting your family.

Those Not in Your Will ... Yet

What happens if you have a newborn child and you do not update your will before you die? Does your new child not get anything in your will because you were not able to update the will in time to include him? Most states have laws that provide for some protection so that your family members can be protected even when you may not have included them in the will.

These are called pretermitted or omitted heir statutes and vary from state to state. They always only include your spouse and your children though. Should you die before you can include them in your will, there are stipulations that allow you to give them something. States mandate, in some cases, that these individuals be given something.

As you have seen, laws can help you during the process of setting up your will, but they can also play a problematic role. Most laws do have good intensions; they just may not be your intentions. You should work closely with your estate planning attorney to find out what you can do in your state to make sure that your wishes are fully carried out, under the letter of the law, as much as you can. Do not assume that you can do anything you want in your will; learn what you can and cannot do so that you do not waste your time.

PROBATE: AVOID IT AT ALL COSTS

You may know what probate is, and if so, you know that you want to avoid it. But do you know what it means and how it works? The fact that you want to avoid probate is a good thing. There is nothing good that can come of it because it costs quite a bit of money, and it is a long, drawn out process. If you can, avoid it by having a good plan for your estate (which is what this book will assist you in doing).

Understanding probate is important because many estates pass through this process. Probate can mean the presenting of a will to a court official so that it can be filed, but it is more commonly a term that is used to describe the process of going through the settling of a will. The process of probate is a long one, but one that happens to many. Here is a brief look at what the process involves:

- Filing the will with the court, usually done by your attorney.

- Determining and inventorying the deceased person's property and estate.

- Determining the need for and having an appraisal of the property done.

- Paying off any money that is owed in taxes or otherwise through the estate, such as paying off debts.

- The will must then be "proved valid," which means that the court has to agree that the will is valid and should be used. In 90 percent of the cases, this is done as a routine manner, unless someone has a valid reason to contest the will, which is rare.

- Finally, the estate is distributed to those that are listed in the will.

It sounds easy and painless, right? If you do not have a will or any other legal means to distribute your property, your estate still must go through probate. If your will is found to be invalid, then you also need to have the estate go through probate.

If a will or an estate has to go through probate, the end result is likely to be a large waste of money and time. Most of the time, there is no need for there to be any long, drawn out process. There is usually no one saying that the will is not valid, and in most cases, the estate will be divided by those that are left behind anyway, so there is no reason to worry about this.

What you will find when you enter probate, if you have to, is that the process is an expensive mess created and maintained by attorneys. Attorneys claim that probate is a process that must be used if they are to protect the heirs as well as to resolve any creditor problems that could threaten the benefits that the heirs should receive. Probate, according to them, protects the deceased person's property and therefore must be used in order to safeguard against any files that are not legitimate or are somehow otherwise wrongfully applied to the estate.

As we have mentioned, this is a rarity, and often it is necessary for the estate to go through probate just to pay attorney fees. Probate is a process that mostly involves some clerical and administrative work that should be done quickly and without this procedure. Yet there is no doubt that probate is a big business right now, and therefore, it is unlikely that we will be able to do without it any time soon. Nevertheless, probate is something that you want to avoid if possible.

Should your estate enter probate, it will likely go through the process for at least one full year. During this time, creditors and others that feel they have a stake in the estate have the right to come forward and say so. Any creditor that does not do so in the amount of time allotted by your state's laws will not be able to collect against the estate once it has filed. Probate is by far one of the longest drawn out legal issues facing people today. If you were to establish a living trust instead of a will to dole out your property, you could complete the process in a matter of just weeks, rather than a full year.

During the probate process, there is a need to have someone that can legally get through the system to help you. You will hire a probate lawyer to handle the process. This person will work toward closing the case, but it means a few court appearances as well as filling in some paperwork. Your estate planning attorney should be able to do this for you, but make sure he or she is okay with helping you get through the process much faster if possible.

You will also need to hire an executor of the will. This is someone in your family or a friend that can help to make sure that your will is carried out the way that you want it to be. He or she is responsible for making sure that your wishes are carried out as much as possible. The executor usually follows the lead of the probate attorney during the process to know what he or she needs to do and what to sign.

THE COST OF PROBATE

One of the hottest issues with those that have to work through the probate system is its cost. Many expenses are tacked on during this process. Many times, the largest costs are the attorney themselves.

Each state has different laws in regards to what attorneys can charge in probate cases. This amount changes based on location; for example, if you live in California, you can expect to pay more than someone living in Wyoming. Yet each state's laws are different in how they figure out this amount as well. In some states, as long as the judge determines that a fee for a probate attorney is "reasonable," it can be charged. In other states, a percentage system is used instead. That means that the attorney receives a percentage of what the estate is valued at.

In any case, the costs are high. It is averaged that the average estate valued at $500,000 will be charged attorney fees for probate at a rate of $10,000 to $20,000. And exactly what do you get for this fee? Usually just a few court appearances and a few documents signed here and there. What is more is that most attorneys make quite a few of these probate cases happen each year.

Still there are other fees. Legally, the executor of the will is entitled to a fee for their services, which is determined again by your state's laws. Since in most cases the estate is passed to the executor of the will after the claim has been filed, most executors often refuse payment. Yet it is still their legal right to accept it.

Another set of fees comes from the actual legal system. There are fees for having the property appraised (that can run you several hundred dollars or more) and fees for court costs (another several hundred dollars). You will find that there are additional fees for filing the paperwork or having a notary sign that paper you must file.

A big mistake to avoid is allowing your attorney to be both the probate lawyer and the executor of the will. This would mean that he or she can claim both amounts of money set aside during the planning of the will (or from the estate) for himself or herself. He or she will not do much to earn those extra funds either.

Do You Have to Have a Probate Attorney?

So, you are sitting there asking yourself if you have to have an attorney to do this work for you, right? One way to cut out the costs of an attorney is to have the executor do the court appearances himself or herself. While this is a good solution and one that could be pulled off by most, the fact is that a few states do not allow it. In other states, judges make it difficult for the executor, which makes them even less effective.

Two states, California and Wisconsin, have a system in place that will allow this. It is called the in pro per action procedure, which is something that you should look into if you live in those locations. This simply means that the executor can stand "in pro per" or represent your estate themselves without the help of an attorney. These states have procedures in place to help individuals do this.

On the other hand, those states that do not have these specific procedures in place but do not have any laws against the process are nearly impossible to benefit from. There are intricate details that need to be completed, and there is not much help for those that are not legally educated. The fact is that if you do not have a lawyer through the process, you will not get much help from judges or other court appointed individuals, which will lengthen the procedure.

You do not necessarily have to have an attorney to help you through the probate process. While that may be the case, you do need to either thoroughly educate yourself by visiting your library, get some help from law books, or have someone help.

AVOID IT IF POSSIBLE

Although skipping the attorney seems like a good option, it is still a risky business and a difficult road to travel. Instead, see if you can at least avoid probate for some of your larger estate pieces and therefore cut the costs down considerably. Avoiding probate, if possible, is the best solution for those looking for reduced fees.

If your estate has a low value, as determined by your state's laws, you may be able to skip probate with a will. But this is rare and is only the case when individuals do not have much property, or debt, upon death. Most wills do need to go through probate. This is why we talk a good deal about other tools available to you to overcome some of the obstacles that probate puts in your path. Avoiding probate through the use of one of these other methods can be a better choice for many of those looking for some financial relief.

If you have the opportunity to do so, transferring as much of your property out of your will into another means to get to those that you love may be one of the best things you can do. It can save you thousands of dollars because most of the other options for leaving your belongings behind to your heirs do not have to go through probate.

To help you make that decision, consider these different types of tools to help you to move your property and estate from your possession into the possession of others.

Joint Tenancy

This is a good tool, and the simplest, to use to move your estate without having to do it through a will. It is also an easy solution for those looking for a way to avoid probate. Joint tenancy is a good solution for those that own property together, such as a long-term married couple.

There are downfalls to this, though. For example, you may be charged a gift tax for doing so. You may also have a better option available to you, such as a living trust which can provide you with a bit more reassurance. Make sure to talk to your tax expert to determine what your state's taxes will be in consideration of this or other tools that you have. Comparing the tax savings here is important.

Living Trust

Another solution is that of a living trust. This tool avoids probate completely and gives you quite a bit of control over your property as you age. You have a good amount of flexibility and you are protected even in cases where you become incapacitated. Therefore, it is a safe and flexible option for transferring your estate to your heirs.

On the down side, a living trust can pose some additional problems. For example, they are more difficult to create. You will need to work with your estate planning attorney (do not worry, his or her fees are less and well worth it) to plan out a thorough plan of action. You may find that this additional cost does tack on some financial expense but again, it can be money that is well invested, too. You will also have to maintain your living trust with your estate planning attorney over time. These trusts do need to be updated and monitored for necessary changes.

Solutions That Are Specific

You may have a few other solutions to consider as well. For example, you can use a Transfer on Death Car Registration that is easy to do and allows you to keep your car out of probate. While it is only available in a handful of states, it is a way to skip probate for vehicles.

The same basic thing can be used if you own securities. You can use a Transfer on Death Registration for Securities to help move them from one owner to the next. The only state that does not allow for them is Texas. Otherwise, it is an affordable and easy way to avoid probate.

Again, if you own real estate, you can use these tools. A Transfer on Death Deed For Real Estate is an excellent tool for those looking to move property without having to have it go through probate. This option, too, is only available in a handful of states; however, looking into it is well worth the time.

Beneficiary Account Set Up

If you have a pension plan, you can have a beneficiary named to that plan that will pay directly to them on your death. This will allow you to avoid probate of your income and it keeps your family taken care of relatively quickly. Make sure that you read through the details of these accounts, though, to find out if there are any limits on what can and cannot be provided for in these situations.

You can also do this with your retirement accounts. By naming a beneficiary, you side track the probate system completely.

Once again, if you want to provide funds for your family that are easily accessible and quickly available to them, take on a life insurance policy. These are excellent vehicles for fast financial help, and proceeds from these policies are not allowed to go through probate. If you can afford it, it is well worth it.

Other Solutions

There are other solutions to avoiding probate. For example, if you live in a common law state, you may have something called a Tenancy by the Entirety. This is an easy to create tool that is only for married people. It allows you to move assets easily, but if there is any issue of your spouse or you becoming incapacitated, you should look elsewhere.

Or you can consider Pay on Death Bank Accounts. These are an ideal option because they do not cost you much to set up and they avoid probate. You can only use your funds in bank accounts and in some government securities, though. It is a solution for those that have cash or securities to be distributed to adults.

These solutions work for many people because they offer the ability to get around the probate system, something that makes sense for most. Yet, there is much more to learn about how to avoid probate, and it is well worth learning about.

Informally Probating Yourself

If your loved one does not have many reasons for going through probate, such as having many assets, it can be possible to avoid probate. For example, if your loved one does not have any debt and has only household items to their name, (or this is your own case) then when the individual dies, the family can come to the home and divide up the belongings without any problem. In this case, there would not be any problem avoiding probate because there is no debt and there is little valuable property.

The only way for this to work is if:

- There is little property that belongs to the individual.

- The family must be able to gain access to all the property of the individual.

- They must agree on how the property will be divided up evenly.

- They must pay any and all creditors without any problems with who will do this.

Informal means like this can be easy to do. If you already know that you would like several people in your family to have certain items, you can make sure they receive it by talking with your family about your wishes and making sure they will honor this. There is not a legal way of dictating this and being 100 percent sure that it will go through as you would like it to, but you can work with your family to determine if a small will happens to be enough.

There are many types of property, though, that cannot go through this type of process. For example, if there is any real estate involved, it is not possible for you to go through this process. There must be a legal authority that can say where the property will be transferred, not just a say so from one of your heirs. If you have other items like anything with a title, then these too cannot go through an informal means. These items require that a legal title change names, which means that lawyers do have to get involved, and often probate must take place as well.

The other problem that occurs with an informal avoidance of probate is that people often do not agree. If you want the living room furniture in your parent's home and so does your sister, the fact is that someone is not going to get his or her way. If there is no way to come to an agreement about how property will be divided, the unhappy party has the right and the ability to file a formal probate, in which case the probate process begins and the costs and the entire process of splitting up the property goes through the process as determined by your state's laws. You are still unlikely to gain anything from the estate that you want in this case simply because of the costs associated with the proceedings.

The solution for you, the person planning on leaving your estate behind, is to have a simple will that does not include much property and does not have any type of property that has a title attached to it. In this case, your wishes must be followed as you define in your will, which will effectively eliminate the problems.

If creditors are not paid off in full, they too can file a formal probate, which would mean that the process of probate can happen so that every element of your property must be taken through the probate process. Therefore, heirs should pay down any and all creditors as much as possible. Or you can prepare to leave some funds behind in savings to pay off creditors as well.

For most, planning to avoid probate means taking a long look at what they need to accomplish. If you are looking to take care of your children, you may not need to worry about planning to avoid probate just yet. Right now, the most important thing for you is to set up the means to care for your family. But if you are aging, now is the time to consider any of the methods that we have talked about to avoid probate. In the next chapter, we will go into more detail on how to do just that: avoid probate through other means.

CAN PROBATE BE A GOOD THING?

There are some times when probate can be a good thing for your heirs. If you have a large amount of debt, going through the process of probate can be a good thing for you. Often, this is the best way for you to settle what you owe and to come out on top.

If you have debts that exceed what would be considered normal every day household costs, you may not want to avoid probate.

Those that have:

- Mortgages

- Car or other vehicle payments

- Credit card debt

- Small debts such as subscriptions

- Utility bills

DO NOT want to file probate.

Those that have:

- Debts that are larger from a business

- Have a failed business

- Have large amounts owed to creditors that you know will come after your home

- Have pending lawsuits or claims against them

DO want to file probate, especially if your will's executor plans to fight those claims. Here, probate can help resolve creditor liability and can handle the legal action that many creditors will use to try to get their slice of your estate pie.

When you die with this type of debt being owed, the creditors have a limited amount of time to let their wishes be known. Sometimes this is as short as four months, sometimes as long as a year. If they do not speak up about their claim on your estate during that time, they do not get to claim any right to your estate. But if they do, then you need probate to help you get through the process.

In addition, if there is any way that you think your estate will be challenged by anyone, then probate can be a benefit to you. For those that know there will be a challenge, probate is a solution because of just how hard it is for the challenger to win his or her case. He or she must show that somehow you have violated laws and therefore should be made to pay him or her some sort of money through your estate. He or she may have to prove that you are incompetent and unable to handle this type of decision making process.

Unless these challengers can attack your will with a legally justified and provable reason that your will should not go through, the challenges will not be given much leeway by judges. But if you do not allow the estate to go through probate, the challenger's time frame is longer for making claims against the estate, and he or she can fight your heirs legally for years about the will and the assets that you have. Therefore, allowing these situations to go through to probate is essential.

What Is Good and Bad about Probate?

Let us take one more look at the good side of probate and the bad side.

- Probate allows your estate to be divided fairly among your heirs as dictated by your state's laws.

- Probate has definite, defined procedures that help to protect you from attacks against your will by creditors or those claiming that your will is not valid.

- Probate helps to provide a transfer of your property that is fair and done correctly, as your will and laws dictate.

- Probate can be costly if an attorney is used and can be more costly than it should be.

- Probate can be a long, drawn out process that will not provide funds to your heirs quickly unless an allowance is used for day to day living expenses.

We will assume that you do not want your estate to go through probate because, although mentioned last, the final two points above are important points to you. Therefore, our recommendation is simple. Protect your assets that are worth any type of real value through another means if possible (which we will cover in a just a bit). In addition, have a backup will that will dictate where everything will go and how it is to be handled. This can be used alongside or at least as a backup plan for your estate.

When you do these things, you can protect your heirs, as well as get them through an otherwise messy and costly proceeding.

WILL SUBSTITUTIONS THAT SAVE YOUR ESTATE

As you know from reading this book, your goal in planning your will is to be sure that your estate goes where you want it to go. But a will is only one option that you have. It is, by far, the most commonly used tool to help you make decisions regarding your estate, but that does not mean that it is the best option for you. There are a handful of products, like will substitutions, that can do a better job of protecting you. Of course, as you have seen from the last chapter, that also includes making sure you do not have to go through probate. But which, if any, of these is the right product for your needs?

We will go through a set of different types of tools and the frequency with which they are used. You should look at several of them and work with your set of power players to make the right decisions. Your attorney, your tax advisor, and your financial planner are key to helping you overcome any possible problem with any of these solutions.

There are many benefits to using will substitutes. For starters, they give you more control over what happens to your estate. For example, you may be able to have more leeway on who gets what even though your state laws say something different. In some of these substitutions you will be able to override what your will says, as well as what your state law dictates, making it the prime tool for determining what happens to your estate.

Why would you want to override your will? There are many reasons. But for the sake of time, let us give an example. Let us say that you write your will to include various elements that are important to you, but you do not have the ability to control your will as much as you would like due to state laws, or perhaps you want to try to avoid probate. Therefore, your will is your backup plan. It may not be what you want, but it is what is in place if everything else falls through.

In addition to your will, you provide a living trust or another of the tools we will mention. Now, your will is overridden (assuming that is included in the language), and your living trust is in place. But should something go wrong there, the will would then hold its own ground. As you can see, this legal maneuvering can be complicated, but with the help of your attorney, it can be simplified.

WHEN TO CONSIDER SUBSTITUTES

When should you consider will substitutions? Here are a number of times and reasons why you may choose to do so.

1. You do not want to waste time. You know that probate is a lengthy process, and if you know that your family will need your estate faster than what probate can provide them, you can establish a means for taking care of them while probate is happening (or even in lieu of it). With several of the will substitutes, property is transferred right away, allowing no one time to have to make ends meet while probate figures out what is going on.

2. You do not want to waste your money. Plain and simple, the cost of a probate attorney alone is reason enough to seek out additional help from these substitutions. There are other laws in place that can be costly to you as well and can be avoided with the help of substitutions for the will. In later chapters we will talk about some new laws that are in place that seem to want to take quite a bit from your estate. But when filing a substitution for your will, the federal government cannot touch these pieces of your estate, and therefore you are protected.

3. You want more control. Many will substitutions allow you more control over what happens to your estate. As we mentioned, you get more say in what happens to your property when you use these tools.

Working with your team of advisors is the best way to determine what tools to use. Special circumstances can often help determine the right course of action for your needs.

WHICH WILL SUBSTITUTE SHOULD YOU CONSIDER?

There are several types of will substitutes that you can use. Some are well worth your time depending on what you need to use them for. To help you, let us break down some of the options that may be right for you.

Your options include: joint tenancy, living trusts, tenancy by the entirety, payable on death accounts, life insurance, and other beneficiary accounts. Each fits a specific case and should be used if you determine it is the right method.

WHAT IS JOINT TENANCY?

Joint tenancy is just what it sounds like. If you have this type of property ownership, both you and others own it with the same amount of ownership. That is to say that if two people own a piece of property it is divided equally among them. If three people own it, then it is divided in thirds and so on. Each person owns the property the same amount.

The key element of joint tenancy is that when you die, the others that own the property with you inherit your share equally. So, if you and someone else own your home and you pass away, they have the Right of Survivorship that joint tenancy provides, and therefore they get the other share of the house that you owned. It does not matter if you have a will and have written that part of your property off to someone else.

Sounds like it is a good thing, right? There are some road blocks we will talk about in just a minute, but know that joint tenancy often works well for those that share property. Family members often do this so that when an elder dies, the property is kept in the family.

With this type of arrangement, the joint tenants that have survivorship rights are those that will be equally held as owners of the property; therefore, if one dies, the other gets the remaining property. But if one of the owners deeds their share of the property to someone else, that new person does not have rights of survivorship and will not get sole ownership of the home.

For example, let us say that you own a home with your spouse and have survivorship rights under joint tenancy. If you die, your spouse gets the remaining part of your home as his or her own. He or she now owns the entire value of the home. But let us say that you decide to give your share of the home to your daughter through a deed. Now, she owns your share but she does not have survivorship rights. Therefore, if she dies before your spouse does, her heirs would get her share of the property, not your spouse.

Why would you use joint tenancy over other types of wills and substitutions? There are some good benefits that can come of it.

- You will save money. It is easy and inexpensive to set up a joint tenancy. Technically you do not have to have an attorney to help you through the process (although having your estate planning attorney help you to determine the right course of action can be a good thing). There is no attorney needed when the joint tenancy comes into play when someone dies, either.

- It is easy for the transfer of the title to happen. The process is simple and straightforward with no question about who the property goes to. If one of the joint tenants that has rights dies, then the other gets his or her share of the property. This can be helpful to many people that want to ensure that his or her property goes to one or several people specifically.

- Debts that you have may be reduced. If you have debts when you die, it is up to your estate representative to pay off those debts before your estate can be closed through probate. As you have learned, though, probate is a long process in which creditors must show that they have a stake in the property. If you own property and there is not enough cash to pay off the debts you owe, your representatives may need to sell property in order to pay them off. But joint tenancy property is not included in this most of the time. That is because this type of property is not part of probate and therefore not subject to the debt. But it is important to note that if you have selected to use joint tenancy to hide from the debts that you owe — and this can be proved — then your property can be considered part of the repayment plan.

- It is fast, easy to do, and it is kept quiet. Unlike probate, joint tenancy is something that is done without public records. You will have to pay the necessary taxes (or your estate will) but otherwise, this is not necessarily part of the probate proceedings and therefore it is private. It is fast to set up and fast to dissolve a joint tenancy as well.

Yet even with all these benefits, there are some definite drawbacks to this type of will substitution that you must know about if you are to find success using it. Working with your attorney you can clearly find out if this is the right choice for you. But let us talk about some of the possible reasons why this may not be the best solution for you.

One of the greatest disadvantages of joint tenancy is the fact that you cannot leave your property to someone else after you have the joint tenancy in place. If you want the other joint tenant or tenancy to share your property with you and you have no intention of wanting anyone else to have any share in it, then this is not a problem. But if you do want someone else to share in it, this is not the route to take.

If you end up being the sole survivor of the joint tenancy, you no longer have any survivors to pass that property down to. Therefore, you must make the decision to do something with the property or set up another joint tenancy with others that will get their share of the property should you die.

When you die, you no longer have any say in what happens to the property. Even if the other survivor has agreed to various stipulations as to what will happen to ownership of the property, you have no way of enforcing that as it is completely his or her decision to do with the property as he or she sees fit.

There are a few tax disadvantages as well. You should work with your tax advisor to fully understand what the tax benefits and tax disadvantages are in this type of will survivorship. Should you have a stepped up tax basis, then you could be paying quite a bit more for your joint tenancy than you thought. This could be a vitally important decision in your outlook for tax planning during estate planning.

Is a joint tenancy the right decision for you? If you are not quite sure, work with your tax advisor and your estate planning attorney to figure out the good and bad for your specific case. You can also consider the other types of will substitutions that we talk about here.

WHAT IS A LIVING TRUST?

Another solution to avoiding the use of a will for your estate needs is to use a living trust. While we will dedicate another chapter of this book to setting one up and how to properly use them in your estate plan, they are a popular choice for those that are considering a will substitution and therefore should be included in this location as well.

A living trust is created while you are still alive and therefore is put in place prior to your death. What goes into this trust? The legal term is that of trust principle. There are two important distinctions here. First, an *irrevocable living trust* is one that you are in charge of for yourself. An *irrevocable trust* is a revocable trust after you have died. In an irrevocable trust, your property goes from your possession into that of your heirs as you determine. The key here is that there is no need for probate to become involved in this process.

At any time before you die you can make changes to your trust or until the trust becomes irrevocable such as if you were to become incapacitated.

Who Is Important to Know?

There are several key people in the living trust, each with his or her own role and his or her own responsibility in making your wishes come true. Let us go through them, one by one, and find out how a trust works.

The Trustor is you, the creator of the trust. The Trustee is the person that legally manages the trust for the income beneficiaries. The Income Beneficiaries are those that will be able to use the trust property. The Remainderman is the individual who receives what is left in the trust after the income beneficiaries receive their portion of the trust. Sometimes, there is a need for a designated person to manage the beneficiaries if there are children that are minors listed as beneficiaries. And a Successor Trustee is a person that you, the creator of the trust, place in charge when you die, if you are the trustee of the living trust.

This person, the Trustee or Successor Trustee, is someone that you should trust and that you know has your best intentions at heart. Most people will select their spouse, their child, or a close, trusted family member or friend to handle this job.

The process of establishing a living trust is not necessarily difficult, but it is something that is drawn out and often requires the help of a skilled attorney. The hardest parts to creating a trust are simple legal jargon issues. For example, working with an estate planning attorney will help you to define what the property in the trust is, who will be in each role in the trust, will help to determine how the trust is amended, and determine how much power the trustee is given, and so on.

Why a Living Trust

There is much more to learn about trusts,. We will go into that in a later chapter, but do not write off the living trust just yet. There are many benefits to using them. This is one of the most used documents by those that want to have something else in place over a will. Here are some of the benefits that you will get from a living trust.

If you have real property, such as real estate and investment properties, you do not want to allow these properties to go through probate, as that would decrease their value substantially. With a living trust, this is not necessary. Each state is different on this ruling, though. Those states that consider property in another state intangible property will not use it in an ancillary probate — others will.

As with a joint tenancy, a living trust allows for protection in the form of privacy. With the use of this type of tool, you and your trustee are the only ones that need to know about it, with the exception of the county recorder where the trust is held. No one else needs to be concerned with it like they would be with probate.

Make sure to talk with your tax advisor on the effects that a trust will have on your taxes. If your state has an inheritance tax, you may be required to provide this income information on your tax return.

But by far there are many other advantages to a living trust that should be considered. For example, the main reason for them is the fact that you can better control what happens to your estate. You have the ability to better plan for your estate and to protect it from probate. You have the ability to predict what happens in the future with better accuracy, and you have the ability to make changes. You can name additional, alternate beneficiaries, and you can name someone to keep your children's interests at heart if you die while they are minors.

If you and your spouse own property together through a living trust and are both named co-trustee and co-trustors, the other gains ownership of the house when one of you dies. There is no need for the home to go through probate. And when that last survivor also dies, the house passes through the living trust to whoever was designated to get it, again avoiding the probate process. If you do not have this in place, the home and property can be subjected to the fees of the probate process twice.

By setting up and managing your trust now, you also allow yourself to see what will happen to your estate when you are gone. For example, if you set up your trust to provide for your heirs to manage your investments and they do not do well with it or become untrustworthy, you can make changes to your trust while you are still alive and, therefore, protect your estate from failure. You can do this with numerous things, such as donations and other distributions, that you set up. If you do not like how they are being handled, you can make changes so that your funds are not being wasted or perhaps you would like to give them more for a job well done.

As you can see, with a living trust, there is an excellent opportunity for you to manage your future even if you are not alive. There are benefits to living trusts, but working with your estate planning attorney and tax advisor is still smart for business.

The Pitfalls of a Living Trust

Like everything else in estate planning, there has to be a down side to a living trust. Yes, there are some disadvantages. While these are important to note, you should consider how they affect you individually.

One of the greatest problems with a living trust is the fact that you have to fund a living trust while you are living, which means that the funds and property need to transfer hands when the trust is put into action. This also means that you have to be able to fund the trust while you are living. This means that each time that your property changes hands, you gain or lose an investment or transfer real estate. For example, the trust has to be updated again. This can pose a real problem, or rather hassle, to those that are investors and make changes regularly.

Another problem arises when you do not put property into the living trust. For example, let us say that you get an inheritance from your Aunt Sue, but you forget to put it into your trust officially. If you do not do this, those funds are considered to be probate required funds because they never were part of the trust. Therefore, they will go through the probate process.

As mentioned, an advantage of the trust is that you can make changes to it readily, but you also have to monitor it for necessary changes as well. You need to decide if the goals of the trust are being met and, if not, make changes that will allow them to be met. If you do not seek out the trust often and update it as necessary, you will not be able to reap the benefits of that trust.

Additionally, living trusts often take longer to have their funds dispersed because they are subject to creditor filings. If a creditor files a claim against your estate for money that you owe to them, the trustee must make sure that it is paid in full. In addition, they must wait a required amount of time (and usually want to do so) to ensure that there are no other claims against the funds. Should they place those funds with the beneficiary that does not do as they should with them and a creditor files a claim, there could be personal liability issues to deal with.

Last, take into consideration the costs of a living trust. Sometimes, a do it yourself living trust will only cost you a small amount. Other times, especially in larger cases, the fact is that a living trust will cost you a large amount to set up and to maintain. You will need to determine what these costs are because of how much they vary from person to person. It is important to work with an estate planning attorney for the design and filing of living trusts. Since it is a legal document that will be null and void if not carefully prepared, it is a safe bet to get help in the process.

A word of warning for you about planners that are trying to sell you on the idea of a living trust: If you are considering purchasing and setting one up because you have been sold the idea, make sure you use a trusted (by you) financial planner and estate planning attorney. Do not go with the ad you saw in the paper. You want to make sure that the costs are not being inflated for their benefit.

There are good and bad aspects of a living trust. If you want to play an active role in what will happen to your estate when you are gone and do it before you die, then a living trust can be a good option for you. If you want to find success in putting a will together and forgetting about it, a living trust may not be for you. With careful planning and execution, though, they can be a good solution for substituting a will. Work with your attorney to determine the right solution for you.

JOINT TENANCY BANK ACCOUNTS

Another option that you have for funding your estate needs is that of a joint tenancy bank account. If you are considering this type of account, you will find some good benefits from it. Like joint tenancy, this form offers the same type of joint holding of the account. Both (or multiple) individuals are in charge of the account, hold equal ownership of it, and can get out of it any time they want to. To get out of it, they simply withdraw the funds that are in the bank account. A bank account serves as the property in this case.

Like a joint tenancy, those that use a bank account have the same bearing upon death. The person that survives the other will then take ownership of the entire account. There is no need for probate with this type of account. And if the bank accounts are under multiple people's names, they each get an equal share of the deceased person's equal percentage evenly.

One down fall to this type of will substitution is the problem of gift taxes. In some locations, joint tenancy bank accounts can be subject to gift taxes, which are simply taxes that you will have to pay when you give a sizable amount of money to someone as a gift. If you want to use this type of will substitute, make sure that you do so with the advice of your tax advisor, as he or she can help you to determine the need for a gift tax.

TENANCY BY THE ENTIRETY

Tenancy by the entirety is another solution for will substitutes, but is only available in a handful of states. It is like that of joint tenancy with one real difference — only spouses can use it. Therefore, you can only have two people holding the joint tenancy.

Like joint tenancy, the rights of survivorship are in play, which means that when one spouse dies, the other will gain ownership of the rest of the property. This also means that there is no need to pass through probate because the tenancy overrules that of any will or state laws that are in place. The property automatically transfers from the deceased spouse's possession to that of the surviving spouse. Another difference is that with tenancy by the entirety, there is no ability to transfer your funds to someone else should you wish to. The only way that this could happen would be through consent or notification of the other spouse.

If you are considering tenancy by entirety (which by the way is sometimes referred to as interests by the entirety), you should work closely with your attorney to insure that it is offered by your state, as well as if it fits your needs the best. Should you divorce, the tenancy by entirety is dissolved and you enter into a state of tenants in common, where your share of the property could be passed down from you to anyone that you would like it to (as through a will).

PAYABLE ON DEATH ACCOUNTS

For those that are considering a simpler method of will substitution, that could be the payable on death accounts. These are not as well known as a living trust or a joint tenancy, but are still good considerations if your situation fits. These types of accounts are just what they sound like. When you set up the account, you simply list who you wish to be your beneficiary on the account.

There are several types of these that can be used for bank accounts, car registrations, and real estate. Each of these payable on death accounts allows you to name someone to claim them when you die. And it can not be made much simpler. In most cases, the individual simply needs to bring in a copy of your death certificate and some personal identification for themselves. He or she takes this information to the title or holder of the account and then is able to transfer the property into his or her name, claiming full ownership of it. Again, there is no need to pass through probate and be taxed as such.

The one important aspect of payable on death accounts that you must realize is that these accounts often require some monitoring. For example, if you have set up a bank account that is payable on death for each of your three grandchildren, you should go back and take a closer look at those accounts every so often. That is because they may earn interest (or otherwise increase in value) at different rates, and therefore, the ending balance may not be what you want it to be. If each child is supposed to receive an equal amount but one account does not perform well, this could be a problem.

Yet the benefit of payable on death accounts is the fact that they are so easy to manage. You can make changes to them at any time, and make any changes that you would like to, until you die. Therefore, you can go in and change the amounts, change who you wish to give the funds to by listing a new beneficiary, and even use the funds if you need and want to. These are some of the most flexible options available because of how fast they transfer and how easy they are to manage.

OTHER WILL SUBSTITUTES

There are a handful of other will substitutes that are available for your use. Each of these is can be useful, even though it may seem simple to use and it may not even seem like it is a will substitute. But using them is a way to sidestep probate and still get the funds and property that you own to your beneficiary as quickly as possible.

Savings Bonds

One solution that you have is that of a savings bond. Yes, the same old bonds that you used to consider purchasing. It is not uncommon for people to purchase them and stash them away for a rainy day (or to leave for their beneficiaries) and accumulate thousands of them. This is a good way to transfer your funds to someone else upon your death, but it is also a way for you to accumulate some interest on the funds that you are socking away. Since bonds double in value over time and are one of the safest types of investments, they are ideal for most individuals to use for their beneficiaries.

There are two types of savings bonds, each with their own benefits. One is called an alternative payee option, which is a savings bond that works much like that of joint tenancy. Both of you are listed on the savings bond, and both of you can cash them in at any time. But when one dies, the other has the full ownership of the bond. This happens through the rights to survivorship.

The other type of savings bond is called a beneficiary payee. In this type of savings bond, there is a beneficiary listed on the bond. When you, the bond owner, dies, the savings bond transfers to the person that you have listed as a beneficiary. In this case, the bond transfers the same basic way that other property would transfer through a will.

You may need to talk to your financial planner and tax advisor about savings bonds. There may be a need for taxes on these bonds, depending on the way that you have them set up. In addition, you should include them as a positive tool in your estate planning.

Retirement Accounts

If you have retirement accounts, you may already have a will substitution in place. Those that are using 401(k)s or even IRAs have a built-in plan already in the works. In most of these types of accounts, the individual that is adding to the account is able to list their beneficiaries or the people that are going to get a share of his or her funds when he or she dies.

For example, if you have a 401(k) set up, as part of that process you will list a beneficiary that will take claim over your account when you die. This allows you to easily provide funds for that person upon your death. Setting up a 401(k) or other retirement account is relatively simple, especially when your employer is sponsoring one.

The only thing that you should take note of about these retirement accounts is the tax implications of them. Depending on the type of account that you have and how and where it is set up, your beneficiaries may need to pay taxes on the funds that they receive. Talk to your tax advisor about the best route to take with these. Also, your financial planner can help you choose the right one for you. There are various retirement oriented investment options out there today that can be quite beneficial no matter where you are in the estate planning process.

Deeds

Deeds are like titles on things like your house and other real property that you own. A deed, though, is a useful tool in estate planning. A deed can be used to move your property from your possession to that of your beneficiary when you die.

There are some tricky aspects to doing this, though. If it is shown that your deed was changed to reflect a property transfer at the grantor's death, this could be shown as a possible problem, and therefore, the deed could be rejected.

With deeds, you will want to work closely with your attorney. There is specific wording that must be included in the deed to make sure that it provides for what you wish it to. You can use these to help you put your house into the hands of your son or daughter, for example, with language written into the deed. Because a deed is legal evidence that real estate ownership is held by someone, it has the power of being a will substitution that is direct and straightforward when written correctly.

If you wish to use these as your means of transferring property, work closely with your estate planner to make this happen. You can do it yourself, but it is a safe bet to work with an attorney that can make sure that your wishes are carried out legally.

SUMMING UP

Now that we have plowed through all the various ways that you can avoid probate, it is still important for you to realize that any of these mechanisms should be backed up with a basic will. As you will see later on, developing an estate that encompasses all your wishes is a process of finding the right tool to make your wish come true. When you have an idea of what options are out there, you can make a good decision about what to do to make that happen.

Although most of these elements can be done by you alone, it pays to work with your estate planning team. They will ensure that you take the right route for your particular situation.

Case Study: David J. Bernstein

The tax laws are not designed to protect your estate. Instead they are designed to take away from your estate as much as possible in order to raise revenue for the federal and state governments. The estate laws of each state do provide some protection to you, but they are

but they are designed to put the rights of your creditors first and your beneficiaries last. A competent estate planning attorney can design your estate plan to minimize taxes and preserve as much of your estate as possible.

As technology has advanced, the process for estate planning has become easier and simpler. Estate planning professionals typically have your estate plan fully in place in just a few days or weeks. The client's time can be minimized to just a few hours.

One of the big mistakes that I see in estate plans is to leave a single dollar to someone who you do not want to leave anything. This is not the right way to do this. It may cost thousands of dollars for the administrator to hire an investigator to track down an estranged heir to deliver the single dollar. The best language is to name the person being left out and state that they are intentionally omitted. Stating the reason could lead to a successful challenge if it is not worded properly, so it is better not to state the reason. Disinherited persons may wish to contest not being included but they must prove that you were incompetent, unaware of your family, your environment, your estate, that there was fraud, mistake, or undue influence at the time you signed the estate plan. Without one or more of these elements they have no hope of winning.

For gifts, the right choice to go with is dependant on what the client wants to see happen. I tell my clients that they do not know how

Case Study: David J. Bernstein

much money they will need to live on for the rest of their lives. If they start giving it away before they die, it may not be available in a time of need. Gifting is typically only best for the very wealthy who know that their financial needs will be met no matter what happens.

There is plenty of hope if planning takes place before your incapacity. You can hand pick who will take over without the interference of any outsider. If no plan is in place at the time of your incapacity, you may find yourself at the discretion of the probate court and a court appointed guardian (who may also be a probate attorney), which could cost your estate tens of thousands of dollars per year.

David J. Bernstein, Attorney at Law
33111 Seneca Drive
Solon, Ohio 44139
440-349-4889
www.estatefacts.com

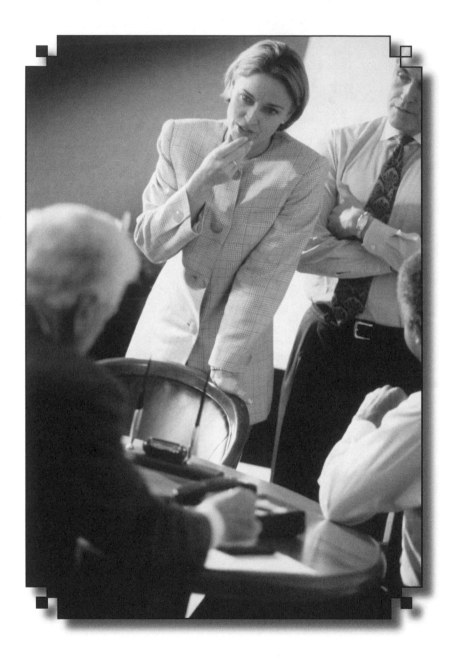

TRUSTS: TRUSTING AND YOUR ESTATE

We mentioned living trusts in earlier chapters, but there is so much to be gained when the right person uses a trust in the right manner for their estate planning goals. If you are considering a trust, though, you should ensure you are working closely with your tax advisor, financial planner, and your estate planning attorney to make it as tight as possible so that your goals are meet throughout the process.

Now, take a minute to go back and read what we have described as a living trust. Once you have done that, you can now move through this section, which gives you some additional information on the advantages of setting up a trust as well as how to set up a trust.

A living trust is a will with one huge benefit: You can use it instead of a will and avoid probate. One important thing to know is that until you die, the property in the trust is still yours to do with what you will. Of course, should you make changes you should go back and change the documentation in the trust to match your requirements and desires. Yet there are many different ways to use a trust besides just the living trust that we have described.

For example, if you have a disabled child, you may be worried about his or her care after you are gone. You can set up a trust for that child that does not just pay out when you die, but continues to care for the child as you have seen fit for years after you are gone. You can also use these trusts to control property that is left to someone else and to provide for your children in another marriage.

A living trust is not the right thing for everyone. Let us clarify that statement. Most people can use and benefit from them, but not everyone needs to use them. For example, if you are young and healthy, the cost of setting up and managing a trust now may be too much for something that you may not later use. In this case, a will can cover the important facts if you should die suddenly. In addition, those that are going through divorce and those that have little property will not find much use for a trust.

Another time when trusts are not necessarily the best tool is when any of the other will substitution devices we have mentioned may work better for you. In addition, those that have debt problems, especially those that are in high amounts of debt or those that are facing legal issues, may want to go through probate to have their creditors limited in what they can claim. Of course, if you do not have anyone that you can trust to manage the trust after you are gone, that too is a reason to not use this type of will avoidance tool. Work with your attorney to determine if a trust is the right thing for your situation.

HOW TRUSTS WORK

We have talked about this a bit before, but let us go through some important points to a trust. You have complete control of your funds in your trust for as long as you are alive. That means that you can have the benefit of moving property and making decisions that are based on what is happening now in your life. And more importantly, once you are gone, the trust can no longer be changed. What you have left there, how you have divided it, and how you have decided it would be used is the way it has to be. Your successor trustee can then immediately hand over the property to the people named as your beneficiary, and within a matter of weeks they could have their property (they must first go through legally changing ownership of the items through documentation).

Now, let us take a quick look at taxes (yes, we know you love them so much so we have dedicated a full chapter for more details). Those that set up a living trust often make the mistake of believing that they have to file a separate income tax return and manage their trust property separately from their other property. This is not the case. The federal government does not recognize a trust until after you are gone; therefore, you will file the same claims that you do now on your property as you will with a trust, all as one.

Trusts and Taxes

Moreover, you still get the same benefits in tax savings that you would on your home when it is included in a trust. For example, if you own a home with a mortgage and place the home into a trust for your child when you die, you still get to reap the benefits of deducting mortgage interest from your income tax form. If you decide to sell your home, you can do so every two years and then exclude some $250,000 of capital gains from taxes, too, (or up to $500,000 for a couple). This is the same thing as having property that is not included in your trust.

Now, you must also take into consideration the estate tax. Do not make the mistake of believing that an estate tax does not have to be paid if you have a trust in place. It quite possibly will still need to be paid even though you are avoiding probate. But you can work with your estate planning attorney to work out a better arrangement that can help you to avoid some of those costly taxes. For example, if you set up a trust that will avoid probate and then in that trust establish another trust that will pay out funds to children or spouses, it will help you avoid some of the estate taxes. This is called an AB Trust. Talk to your estate planning attorney on how this works in your state.

TRUSTS FOR COUPLES

You do not have to be single to use a living trust effectively. It is still one of the best tools for you to use when it comes to will avoidance for couples. In most states, "couples" refers to any set of two people. Although it usually refers to spouses, it does not always have to be so. Or if it offers better advantages for you, each of the individuals in a marriage can have their own individual trust established, with benefits from them. This works the best when there is property that is divided between the two as opposed to having mostly shared property.

If you have shared property, you do not want to go with an individual trust because that would mean dividing up any shared property among the two of you. On the other hand, if you have shared property and individual property as well, you can include both in the trust. In this example, you can have separate beneficiaries listed for your share of the property.

When you have this type of trust established, when the first spouse dies, his or her share of the trust property is spilt apart and given to whoever he or she lists as his or her beneficiaries. Most of the time, this is going to the surviving spouse or children, but whoever he or she has listed as their beneficiaries will get their share of the trust.

CREATING THE TRUST

Now that you have some more information about trusts, it is time to determine if you should use one. Let us break down the questions that you have to ask to determine if it is the right tool for you. You have to determine what you will put into the trust and who you will name as your successor trustee, your beneficiaries, and how debts will be paid once the trust is put into place.

What Property?

First and foremost, what property will you include in your trust? Most people want to include as much valuable property in their trust as possible; therefore, keeping it from going through probate. Unless you have some other way of avoiding probate for your more valuable property, it should be put into a trust. If you establish another means of doing this, the property does not need to enter into the trust as well.

You can use a trust for some of your property and allow other will substitutions to work for the rest. For example, you may have already established a pay upon death bank account for your son; therefore, this does not need to be entered into the trust.

If you put real estate into your trust, there is the benefit of possibly avoiding reappraisal of your property. For example, if you live in a state that requires an appraisal be done if a new owner is placed on the title, this could be costly if you were to move from your current situation into, say, a joint tenancy agreement. However, if you instead include it in your trust, there is no need for this change to happen. That is because the government does not recognize the trust as being separate from you until you have died.

Also important to note is your standing with your mortgage. Sometimes individuals worry about what happens to their mortgage when they place their property into a living trust. Do not worry; because the federal government does not recognize the trust while you are alive, you do not have to do anything with your mortgage when you place your home into your trust.

You do not need to notify your mortgage company. Federal law also prohibits the transferring of your home into a trust from being a reason to "call" the mortgage due. Your insurance company also does not need to be notified. If you do notify them, you may have an increase in your rates. Telling your mortgage company or insurance company only creates hassles for you. Do not bother with the struggle.

Who Will Be Your Trustees?

Now that you should have a good idea of what type of property you want to place in your trust, you need to now name your trustees.

- Who will you name as the initial trustee?

- Who will you name as the successor trustee?

As for the initial trustee, that is usually you. If you and your spouse will enter into the trust together, you can both serve as co-trustees, having equal shares of ownership in the trust. Being the trustee of your trust is important because it provides you with the power to manage your trust until you die.

Technically, you can name someone else as the initial trustee, but that may not be the best route for most individuals. You will have to go into a complicated process that often has legal implications. In addition, you will need separate trust records, and a trust tax return will need to be filed with the Internal Revenue Service. This process is costly and long, but if you want to do it, talk to your estate planning attorney about it first.

Or you can name several people as co-trustees of the property. If you cannot or do not want to manage your property while you are alive, you can set up the trust so that you and others are listed as co-trustees, which helps to circumvent the IRS and still allows you to pass control of your property to someone else.

Next, you need to pick your successor trustee. Your successor trustee takes over for you once you have died. If you are a co-trustee with your spouse, your successor trustee will take over when both of the trustees have died. The successor trustee is responsible for managing and distributing your trust to your beneficiaries after you are gone. You should also include an alternative successor trustee. If your successor trustee should no longer be able to serve as your trustee after you have died or even dies before you, the alternative will take over.

The successor trustee has a simple job, especially when everything has been clearly defined for him, but there is a bit more to the process than just what has been included here. He or she will be responsible for getting several copies of your death certificate and will need to have copies of the living trust. He or she will have to provide for documentation of the trust, his or her identity, and the death certificates to make claims on the property and funds as described in the trust. Do not worry, though; financial institutions deal with successor trustees all the time, and there is no real problem for those that have to do this.

Another responsibility that he or she has to take on is that of preparing documents that need to have title transfers or other such elements. For example, he or she will need to help prepare documents for real estate transfers, which will include helping to get the title transferred, signing for it, and also recording the transfer with your county's public records office.

Of course, the successor trustee also must make sure that home furnishings and mementos are distributed as you have declared in your trust. If you decided that your $100,000 painting collection should go to your third cousin, then your successor trustee must make sure that those paintings end up in your third cousin's hands.

Your trustee will need to notify your beneficiaries of your death and that the trust has become irrevocable (which means it can no longer be changed because you have died). Some states make this a legal requirement. Your estate planning attorney will be able to help you make this happen. Notifying the beneficiaries that the trust is irrevocable, who the successor trustee is, the date that the trust went into effect, and a statement that allows the beneficiary to receive a copy of the trust should be provided to all beneficiaries listed in the trust. Doing this keeps the successor trustee out of lawsuits.

Who Are Your Beneficiaries?

Your beneficiaries are those that will receive your property through the trust. You can name your spouse, your children, or anyone that you would like to in your trust to receive all or part of your property. Your beneficiaries will be listed for only your half of the trust and your co-trustee will be able to list their beneficiaries, too, if a couple forms a trust. They do not have to be the same.

While you do not have to tell your beneficiaries that you are including them in your trust and what they will get, this often makes the job of the successor trustee much easier. As we have talked about, it is important to keep an open dialog between you and your beneficiaries so that they know exactly who will get what. This helps to dissipate problems and hurt feelings later. With a trust, you can make any changes that you find are necessarily throughout your lifetime.

Work with your attorney to determine if there is any need to create an AB trust, as described earlier, or other types of trusts that may have additional benefits for tax breaks. In addition, you may have special needs cases, such as property, that needs to be managed for minor children until they are old enough. When included in your trust, special language is needed to ensure that your beneficiaries receive what they should get, but with special consideration of their needs and yours.

Naming your beneficiaries is one of the toughest jobs you have, but it is a process that can be changed and tweaked over time.

How Will Debt Be Handled?

If you place most or all your debt in a living trust, there may be a problem with paying off any debts that you have. Like most people, you may have promised yourself that there is no need to worry about debt because you plan to have everything paid in full when you die. All good intentions do not always play out. If you end up in the hospital with costly medical bills, how will they be paid? If you die suddenly and your house is still mortgaged, how will this be paid? Handling debt questions now while setting up your living trust is important.

In most cases, a mortgage is not a problem because the mortgage will pass on to whoever you have left the house to. Most people do not leave behind substantial debt when they die. However, if you do there is the need to make some amendments. In standard practice, your successor trustee will pay off all the debts that you have using the property in the trust before it is given out to anyone. It is wiser to have a specific amount set aside in the trust to make these types of payments so that everyone gets what they where supposed to.

You should also monitor your living trust while alive and the value of it in relation to your debt. In estate planning, you want to figure in the debt as part of your estate plan so that no one else has to pay it out of their share of your estate.

MAKING YOUR TRUST VALID

One of the most important things for you to consider about a trust is whether the trust is valid. In the wording and the structure of the trust, you will need to set up and maintain this aspect of the trust. Again, working with your attorney is a must for this reason alone. Even if you do hire an attorney, you should still understand how a trust is set up so that it is valid and will do what you wish it to do.

Step 1: Preparing the Documents

Do not be fooled into thinking that there is a "one way is the only way" philosophy when it comes to creating a living trust document. The fact is that there is no legal form that must be used. Working with your attorney, a simple form can be created that will include what the document is and defines all the terms of the trust. All the important individuals that we have talked about, from the trustor and the successor trustee, down to the beneficiaries, need to be spelled out. You need to identify all your property in the trust and where it will go (and how) to your beneficiaries. Although no witnesses are required, you should have it notarized, which means signing the trust in front of a notary. It is imperative that you do have it notarized, rather than using bank guarantees or other options.

Step 2: Transferring to the Trustee

Next, you need to transfer the trust property into the trustee's name. If you do not make this formal step, the successor trustee will not be able to perform their duties to the fullest. What this means is simply assigning your name to all documents in a specific format. It should read, "John Doe, as trustee for John Doe Trust" on the documents.

The property that will be placed into your trust that has a title or otherwise has legal paperwork that shows its ownership is the first type of property to make this change with. This includes your real estate, bank accounts, your vehicles, your safe deposit boxes, your stocks and bonds, your partnerships, including corporations and limited partnerships, your mutual funds, and your money market accounts. All these have a title or ownership papers that need to be transferred into the trustee's name as we have described.

Some property does not have any such documentation for ownership. Your jewelry, your household items, your clothing, your cash, and any other type of valuable property that you will be placing into your trust without documentation for ownership still need some additional note. To transfer these items into the trustee's name, you will simply include them in a list format on your paperwork with a "Notice of Assignment" listed with them, which simply transfers ownership.

Step 3: Maintaining Your Trust over Time

Just setting up your trust is not enough to keep it going. The trust is unique from most other forms of wills and substitutions because at any time it can be revoked or otherwise changed to fit what is happening now in your life. Therefore, it does take some effort to maintain your trust. But that is not a bad thing.

If you acquire additional property that you want placed into your trust, make this necessary change. If you sell off property, or want to remove it from your trust, this needs to be changed as well. You may also want to revisit your trust often to make sure that the amount that you have left to your beneficiaries is accurate. For example, one account can suddenly increase in value more so than the other, and if you wanted them to be equal, you may need to make some changes to the trust to show this. In addition, life style changes such as the addition of children, divorce, marriage, or other aspects need to be updated as soon as possible.

If you have a shared trust, though, this will need to be updated not just by you but also by your co-trustee or spouse.

Some important notes to consider in regards to maintaining your trust include:

- Amending your trust is a right that you have until your death. You can amend the documents by having amendments added to the document which have been signed by you and witnessed by a notary. Amendments work well for making small or simple changes such as adding your beneficiary to the document or moving one piece of property to the trust. But when large changes need to be made, revoke the old trust and install a new one. It is easier.

- You can add additional property to your trust, of course. When you do this you should be transferring it into the trustee's name, adding it to your living trust documentation with signature and notary, and naming the beneficiary. You may need to make changes to what you already have in your trust if you deem it necessary in allocated assets to your beneficiaries.

- Your trust property can be sold or even refinanced during the time that you own it. You can do so by selling it right out of the trust or you can transfer it back into your sole name from the trust name, and then sell it. You may need to work with a title company for real estate transfers to ensure that the correct method is used. You should then amend your living trust documents to show the changes that you have made.

- You also can completely revoke the trust. If you decide to do this, you will simply provide a signed and notarized document that says so. Sometimes you do need both spouses to sign for this, but more often only one has to make this change.

ABSTRACT OF TRUST

As we have talked about in this section, you would be setting up a trust by spelling out exactly what is to happen to your property after you die.

But what if you do not want everyone to know what your trust will include until after you die? An Abstract of Trust is a type of trust that can be used to accomplish this. This tool allows you to say that your trust exists and that it is going to be used, but it simply is a "short list" of what is included in that trust, rather than spelling it all out.

You may want to do this if a financial institution wants to have documentation that a trust exists, but you do not want to provide them with any details, which legally you do not have to do. Therefore, an Abstract of Trust is formed. In some states, this document is a specific form that must be completed, whereas in other states it is not. When you work with your estate planning attorney, you will be better able to make sure that the right forms and documentation are provided to draw up this type of trust.

SUMMING UP

Now that you have had the opportunity to explore the world of a living trust, you may be ready to dive right in. Before you do that, make sure that you work with your team of advisors in making the decisions that will affect your trust as well as the rest of your estate plan. For many people, the wisest decision is to create a living trust as part of the estate plan, but not as the only part of that estate plan. Finding the right solution for you will take a few more minutes. In the next chapters, we will help you to develop a total estate plan that encompasses everything that you need and want to include.

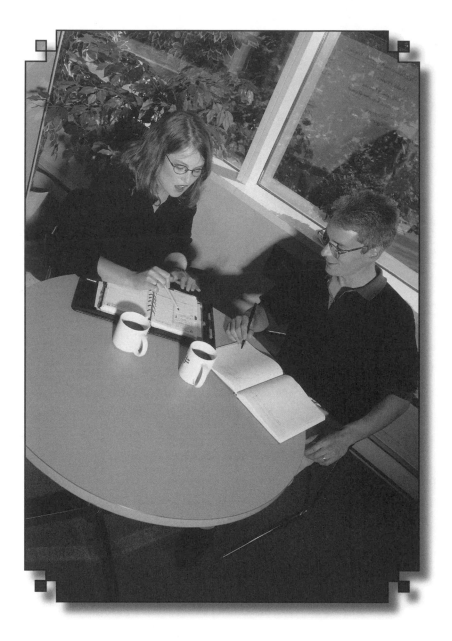

TAXES: ESTATE TAX AND OTHER TAXES

O ne of the largest and most complex areas of estate planning is the tax involved with it. Estate tax is an important part of planning your estate because it will take a large chunk of money from what you leave to your heirs. There are several types of taxes that will need to be planned for and minimized if possible. These include:

- Federal Estate Tax

- State Estate Tax

- Inheritance Tax

- Gift Tax

As part of the planning for your estate, you need to take into consideration each of these types and make changes or allotments to your estate to accommodate them.

Anyone that is living in the U.S. or is a U.S. citizen is required to pay federal estate taxes. All your property in the U.S. is taxable. Yet there are some strange laws in place to determine how much you need to pay if you need to pay. In the last several years, Congress has passed new laws that define this information. Here is what you need to know:

- If you die in 2007 or 2008, you have a personal exemption of $2 million at the highest death estate tax rate of 45 percent.

- If you die in 2009, the amount of personal exemption rises to $3.5 million at 45 percent.

- If you die in 2010, there is no estate tax as it is repealed.

- In 2011, it comes back with an amount of personal exemption at $1 million unless the repeal is held by Congress before this time. Your death estate tax rate is at 55 percent in 2011.

You are not the only one to think that this law is somewhat strange, and it makes estate planning in the long-term somewhat of a problem. What makes it difficult is the inability you have of planning for each situation, and even if you did, at 2011, there would be no way of knowing what happens next. There are political as well as economic reasons for the use of this tax, and therefore, there is no way to know which way it will go.

What should you do? Most estate planners and tax professionals will tell you to plan your estate the best that you can through 2009 for federal estate taxes. It will need to be revised after that point, though.

The first step is to understand and plan for these taxes. You also must determine if you owe them. Let us take a closer look at some of points you need to fully understand.

FEDERAL ESTATE TAX EXEMPTIONS

For most people, there is no need to worry about this tax because the value of your estate is not large enough to be touched. There are several exemptions that you can take into consideration for your estate plan. Here is a breakdown of them.

Personal Exemption

As mentioned earlier, there are exemptions for how much your property is valued at. This will depend on the year in which you die. For those that die before 2009, this is $2 million. In 2009, it rises to $3.5 million, and so on. You can leave this much property to anyone and not have to pay any taxes on it through the federal government. One important note is that if you leave gifts that are taxable during your lifetime, this reduces your exemption amount.

Marital Deduction

Another deduction that you may qualify for is that of marital deductions. This means that all property you leave to your spouse, if they are a U.S. citizen, is exempt from taxes. If they are not a U.S. citizen, this deduction does not apply. This deduction does not change year to year as in the personal exemption. You must be legally married for this exemption to be used. In addition, terms like "significant other" or "mates" are not recognized by this deduction.

Yet there is a potential problem with this. If you die and leave all your property to your spouse, he or she now has increased their personal property, which could push them above the personal exemption allowable (called the estate tax threshold) tax limit. The best way around this is to take steps to plan your estate with this in mind, making sure that both spouses can benefit from it.

You can avoid this tax trap by planning an AB trust for your needs. In this case, each of the spouses places all (or most) of their property into the trust. When one spouse dies, the surviving spouse still has access to the trust property and can use it as needed, but they never own the property outright, which means that they do not have to pay taxes on it.

If you are married to a non-citizen, it is important for you to consider the best route to take in leaving property to your spouse. There are several ways around the rule that you cannot leave them property. First, if the property is under the exemption threshold, you can leave it to them without fear of taxes taking it all. You can also create a "Qualified Domestic Trust" for them. These trusts are complex and the use of an estate planning attorney is important.

Charitable Deductions

For those that are rather wealthy, it may be important and one of the best routes to take to use charitable deductions for what they leave. Gifts to charities are tax exempt, assuming you give them to a recognized tax exempt charity. You will want to work with an attorney to help you set up a "Charitable Remainder Trust." Before you die, you will need to make a gift to a charity. Then, you will receive a certain annual income from the gift property while you are alive. You will need to pay income tax on this throughout your lifetime.

STATE ESTATE TAX AND INHERITANCE TAX

The state takes another look at your tax situation and then assesses their claim to your property when you die. There are two types of taxes to consider here: state estate tax and inheritance tax.

Inheritance Tax

Only some states use this tax:

- Connecticut (which will be phased out by 2008)

- Nebraska

- New Jersey

- Ohio

- Oklahoma

- Pennsylvania

- Tennessee

This tax is for all property that is left by a state resident no matter where that property is located, and all real estate within the state no matter where the property owner died is taxable.

In order for you to learn what these taxes are, you do need to invest in a bit of research or the help of your estate planning team. Each state has a bit of a different situation and varying rules that must be followed. Indeed, there are ways to work around the amount of taxes you need to pay, which your attorney will help you do per your state's laws.

State Estate Tax

Because of the decrease in the federal estate tax laws as mentioned, many states have now implemented new laws in the form of state estate taxes. Before 2005, states used to have a "pick up" tax, which is a tax that they received as part of the federal estate taxes that were assessed to the estate. But, under these new laws, this is no more. Because the need for these funds is still there, many states have created their own state estate tax.

Again, each state has their own unique system for state estate taxes, with their own percentages and exemptions.

GIFT TAX

In an effort to avoid people giving away all their property before they die and avoiding any estate tax by doing so, Congress developed the gift tax to stop them. Gift tax rates are the same as estate tax rates. What is more, this tax is applied not to the recipient of the gift, but to the person that is giving the gift.

As we mentioned, the estate tax is in the process of being repealed and starts again in 2011. While your estate tax exemption rate will change as determined by those laws (see federal estate tax), the gift tax exemption stays at $1 million. This means that those who die before 2010 will be able to leave more property without giving it as a gift at the tax free rate.

Another important part of this tax is to understand when it affects you. If you make a gift that is taxable, you do not pay the tax on it at that time. Rather, you will pay the tax when it is deducted from your estate tax exemption.

There are also several exemptions available for gift taxes. These can help you lower the amount of tax you end up paying.

Annual Exemption

Laws provide you with an exemption amount on a per year basis. For example, this is currently $11,000. You can give away $11,000 per year tax free, and this does not change with the next estate tax laws. If you are married, both members can give separate $11,000 gifts.

This is a per person law. For example, you can give $11,000 to your daughter and another $11,000 to your son. This is called gift splitting, where you will be splitting the gift that is given. For example, if you and your spouse give a gift of $16,000 to your sister and give another $18,000 to your brother-in-law, you would have gone over the $11,000 gift limit per person if it was given singly. But since you split this (or you each gave half) it is considered that you each gave your sister $8,000 and your brother-in-law $9,000. Neither of these is over the limit.

If you are younger, you can give away a considerable amount of your money and property this way. You should also take note that, as the cost of living rises, this gift tax exemption is likely to rise as well. But the cost of living must have a cumulative raise in the current exemption by more than $1,000 before it will rise to $12,000.

Marital Exemption

Any gift that you give to your spouse is tax exempt no matter how much it is. As part of the marital exemption for federal estate tax, this law is in effect. Again, if you are not legally married or married to a U.S. citizen, this is not allowable. For those that are married to someone that is a non-citizen, you can give up to $117,000 per year to them, without any taxes. By giving your non-citizen spouse this sum over the course of time, you can effectively leave them with a tax free estate.

Medical Bills and School Tuition

Another exemption that you may qualify for is when you pay someone else's medical bills or their school tuition. To use this type of exemption, though, you must pay the provider of the service directly. If you give the funds to the student, for example, it no longer is tax free even if he or she uses it to pay his or her tuition. In addition, if the student has already paid for his or her education, you cannot reimburse them for the funds for tax savings. You also cannot pay for things like room and board — just the cost of tuition.

GSTT — GENERATION SKIPPING TRANSFER TAX

Another type of tax that you should take into consideration is the GSTT, or the Generation Skipping Transfer Tax. This tax came to be due to the number of people that were skipping their children and leaving their property to their grandchildren. In doing so, they avoided taxing their property two times (once when passed down from grandfather to son and then second from son to the grandson). This new tax is a large one and effectively stops most people from avoiding taxes in this manner.

If you do want to leave funds in this manner, work closely with your estate planning attorney, who will lower the GSTT amount that you have to pay. This is a complex method of estate planning and one that is best left to the attorney. For those that have a sizable estate, this may be an important consideration.

ESTATE RECOVERY ACT

Although the Estate Recovery Act is not a tax, it is important to mention here as it involves your estate's funds. If you are someone that has used Medicaid benefits throughout your life, you need to consider how it will affect your estate when you are gone. In 1993, Congress passed a new law; this act provides for repayment of Medicaid benefits for certain individuals. That means that if you drew on these funds, you may have to pay them back.

The hardest part to swallow of this act is that most people who have to use Medicaid have less property or assets. For many, the only value comes through with the home that they own.

Some states have a homestead exemption or personal residence waiver that you can use as an exemption to this act. Each state has a different type of exemption here, if they have one. These exemptions can mean the difference between losing the family's home or not. If you draw on Medicaid for any reason, find out if you are one of the likely people that must repay it after death. If so, work with your estate planning team to protect your assets from this repayment if possible.

HOW IS INHERITED PROPERTY VALUED?

Although it is not specifically related to taxes, you are wondering where all the dollars and cents come in. How is your property valued to determine where it stands as far as estate tax goes?

The Tax Basis is the value that is assigned to the property from which taxable gain or loss on a sale is determined. This means that when property is purchased, its basis is usually the cost. For example, let us say that you purchase something valued at $10,000, and then sell it for $21,000. The sale price ($21,000) minus the basis ($10,000) gives up the taxable gain on the asset (in this case, $11,000). In accordance with this, the original cost basis will be adjusted up, such as for improvements, or down, for depreciation. If you made improvements to your home that increased its value, the improvement value is added to the basis of the property. In loose terms, capital improvement is anything that lasts for over one year.

Now, when you take this into consideration with estate tax, note that federal tax laws say that the basis of inherited property is raised to the fair market value of the property at the time of the deceased owner's death. Up or down, it is determined what the fair market value of the property is.

When more than one person owns the property (joint tenancy property) only the portion of the property that is owned by the person that dies is raised or lowered to fair market value. The others will continue to have the same basis of value that they had originally.

What does this mean for estate planning? In almost all cases, it is more desirable to hold on to appreciated property until after you die and allow it to pass through ownership after death. This way, those that inherit the property will have the benefit of the raised value of the property. If it is sold prior to this, there would be capital gains taxes that would need to be paid, plus income taxes to the state. But if your property is sold after your death, there is no tax assessed on it.

You cannot use this formula for calculating gifts that are made during your lifetime. Only property that changes hands after death will qualify for it.

Now that you understand a bit more about what taxes are out there, it is time to take a closer look at how you can reduce what has to be paid.

LOWERING YOUR FEDERAL ESTATE TAXES

It would be nice if you did not have to pay any federal estate taxes (or any taxes for that matter). Yet we all realize that dream is not going to happen. The next best thing to do is to consider how you can reduce what you have to pay in federal estate taxes.

If you believe that your estate will need to pay estate taxes, it is important to do all that you can (within legal restraints) to avoid paying high tax rates. In most cases, you will not be able to avoid all your taxes or even most of them. For those that are very wealthy, there are always strings and loopholes to be found, but an overpriced attorney will be necessary for this (even good financial planning attorneys will point you down the clear path rather than one filled with risky maneuvers).

There are two situations in which anyone can reduce the estate tax they pay:

1. Make gifts during your lifetime.

2. Use an irrevocable trust.

MAKING GIFTS DURING YOUR LIFE

One of the first and best ways to lower what you have to pay is to have less to pay on. If you give away your property while you are still alive, you will remove any potential tax on that estate after your death (you no longer own it after all). There are several things to consider here. Let us break them down.

Federal Gift Tax Exclusion

You can make gifts up to $11,000 per person per calendar year which is considered tax free. When you use this method to reduce your taxes, you will remove a substantial amount over the course of time (you can give away more than $11,000 per year, if you give it to several people). If you have children, grandchildren, or others that you would like to provide funds for, this is an ideal way of making that happen.

In addition to these gifts, you can also give gifts of any amount to other causes. This includes giving payments for someone's medical costs or their tuition. You can also give away your property in any amount to tax exempt charities.

Interest in a Family Business

In some situations, if you give some minority interest in a family owned business to someone, this can reduce your taxes. A minority value is less than that of the value of a majority interest, which will keep it undervalued. Because of the minority business discounts that are available, it can be valued much lower.

In addition to this, realize that it will only work for an exiting business, not one that you create and place major assets in (such as your home). If the business is designed solely to reduce estate taxes, it will not work.

Life Insurance

Another way to lower your estate taxes is through life insurance. If you have life insurance policies at the time of your death, the benefits from the policy will be included in your estate's taxable property. If this policy is large enough and adds too much to your exemption rate, then there could potentially be large amounts of taxes applied to it. On the other hand, though, if you do not own the policy but someone else does, the funds are not subject to tax.

In order for this to happen, the gift of insurance must be made at least three years before you die. No death bed gifts can be made simply because of the potential tax savings.

These gifts are subject to gift taxes. The worth of the policy is the current value of it. This is much less than what is paid at the time of death. In addition, if the present value of that insurance is less than $11,000, once again, there is no tax here.

The question is how do you make this happen? One way to do so is to simply give the policy to another person. You will need an assignment form from your insurance company. Or you can use an irrevocable life insurance trust that will transfer ownership to the other person. If you do not have someone specific to transfer funds to, you should consider a life insurance trust.

There are some disadvantages to using this type of gift to avoid estate taxes. If you sign your life insurance over to someone, you no longer can make changes to it. You cannot cancel it either. Consider how this will affect your needs.

AB TRUSTS

Next, consider the AB Trust. We mentioned it earlier, but let us go into a bit more detail here. If you are a well off couple and know that your shared estate property will push you too far over the estate tax threshold in valuation, you may want to consider this trust. While it will not stop you from paying your estate taxes, it will lower how much is paid in total by both of you.

There is a set amount of estate value that you can have before you are pushed over the threshold and must pay taxes on it. This amount varies per year and may even be repealed altogether. Nevertheless, it is important to understand how this will play a role.

Let us say that you leave your estate to your spouse when you die. The value of the living spouse's estate can rise significantly at this time and therefore push them over the threshold and into taxes. This means that the tax will then need to be assessed against your funds as well as theirs when they die. This is sometimes called a second tax. This lowers the total amount that will pass down to your heirs when both spouses are gone.

With an AB Trust, you can avoid some of this tax without having to split your property apart from each other when one passes away. In an AB Trust, your assets and your spouse's are kept separate, but the surviving spouse is able to use the property in the trust as they need and want to for basic needs and for health care. But they do not gain ownership of that property.

In order for an AB trust to be established, it will require the transferring of most or all the property of each spouse into a separate trust. Usually, this is done with the help of a living trust that spans over both spouse's trusts. While you both are alive, the property is in the living trust and can be changed at any time. However, there are two separate trusts under the living trust that divide the property among the two spouses. Placing all this property into Trust A is step one.

When one spouse dies, the living trust property is split into two separate trusts. Trust A is the deceased spouse's trust. This trust becomes irrevocable. The other trust is Trust B, which is the surviving spouse's living trust.

This is one of the best ways of managing trusts because there is no way to know which spouse will die first. Both will create a Trust A, but only one will go into action. In the creation of these trusts, the "life beneficiary" of the trust is named as the other spouse. This inclusion allows for the other spouse to take use of the property in Trust A for his or her own needs. It does not provide ownership of this property to the spouse, though, which is the key factor in avoiding estate taxes.

In doing this, the life beneficiary has the right to use the property in the trust, to receive all income from the property, and to spend the trust principal for health, support, maintenance, and education as a method of maintaining their current life style.

In addition to this, each spouse will name beneficiaries on his or her AB Trust. After both individuals are gone, the final beneficiaries are used to divide property. In addition, there must be a trustee in place that will manage and watch over the trust. In most cases, this will be your spouse. When one dies, an alternate successor is assigned to Trust A and Trust B.

What Are the Benefits?

Is all this work in establishing an AB Trust worth it? In most situations, it will work for several key situations. If you want to leave most of your estate to your spouse, it works well. If you have a combined estate (with your spouse) that is valued over the estate tax threshold, it can be beneficial.

Those that have a good deal of wealth should consider them. Elderly couples that will likely not outlive each other by many years should also consider them, as they will reduce the amount of estate tax that will need to be paid. Yet it is important that several key understandings be in place as well for a trust to work.

Both spouses, as well as the final beneficiaries, should understand and agree on the trusts and how they are set up. The goal of them is to save money through avoidance of estate taxes and to allow for the surviving spouse to have full use of the property they both own. It is necessary for the entire group to understand that the property in the trust is for the surviving spouse's use and benefit above all else. In that, it is important for final beneficiaries to realize that the estate tax reduction will benefit them, not the property owners.

If the surviving spouse does need to use the funds in the trust to maintain their life style or to pay medical bills, the beneficiaries must agree that this is okay and allowable. For situations in which there will be conflict between the surviving spouse and the final beneficiaries, an AB Trust can just make it worse. The surviving spouse has the right to use and benefit from what is left in the trust by their spouse who has died. In that, if the final beneficiaries want the funds to be left alone, this can be cause for conflict.

There are some people that may not benefit from an AB Trust. Others do not want to leave a large amount of property to the other spouse; therefore, they can determine where the property goes in other documentation. Then, there are those that need much more extensive help for their estate plans.

Couples that are middle-aged may also not benefit from it. If the surviving spouse lives many years longer than the other, this could cause a number of problems for him or her. Also, those that have one spouse that is much older than the other may have this problem.

Is This Right for You?

There are a few reasons why you may not want to consider AB Trusts, even though they seem to provide some of the best estate planning for those with estates over the tax threshold. Take some time to meet with your financial planning attorney to go over the process and the benefits. Both of you should understand what is happening and agree that it is the right choice for you. You will also want to consider a few things that may push you away from this type of estate plan.

For example, there will be some limitation on the property that is left behind to the surviving spouse. While they can use it to maintain their current life style and for health and education, they still cannot spend the funds left in the trust any way that they want to. You must be legally allowed to use those funds for the purpose you intend.

Of course, there are fees for these trusts that must be taken into consideration. Your estate lawyer will draw up what these fees will be. Yet you will need to have just that, an estate planning attorney. He or she will be required to divide the couple's property as equally as possible, which will take some work. In addition, you will need a tax payer ID for the trust because the surviving spouse will need to file an annual income tax return on the trust.

For many, the hardest part of the process will be to maintain accurate records of the trust and its property. This means that the surviving spouse will need to maintain their own property as well as the property that is in the trust. They must be kept separately as well.

When everyone understands the process and the requirements of AB Trusts, they can be beneficial to those that are using them, especially as a tax advantage.

IS THERE ANYTHING ELSE?

If you are still looking for a few more ways to lower the cost of the estate taxes that you pay, there are just a handful of other options. Let us reveal them here.

QTIP Trust

A Qualified Terminable Interest Property Trust is one option that you have. This trust does not reduce or stop estate taxes, but it does postpone them. It can be used when an individual estate exceeds the estate tax threshold. Let us say that you die and leave behind $500,000, which is over the estate tax threshold. You can leave this behind in the QTIP Trust, which will delay the payment of the estate taxes. The benefit of the QTIP Trust is simple. It provides for the use of the property by the surviving spouse throughout their lifetime but also qualifies for the marital deduction that we talked about. That means that when the spouse who creates the trust dies, the property is not taxable. In addition, the QTIP allows the individual creating the trust to choose the final beneficiaries.

The estate tax on this property is assessed when the surviving spouse dies, as it is now part of their property. But what is important to note is that the taxes are assessed based on the value of the assets when the surviving spouse dies, not when the first spouse dies. This can significantly raise the value of the property and therefore cause additional tax requirements to be paid.

To consider using a QTIP Trust, talk with your financial planner and lawyer about the benefits in your specific situation, as this is a complex type of trust that requires an in depth consideration.

Life Insurance Trusts

A life insurance trust is one that you may set up to help you to avoid estate taxes but has to be done in a specific manner. This is an irrevocable trust, meaning that it cannot be changed. The trust will own life insurance that you currently own. By transferring your life insurance to the ownership of the trust, you secure the funds before you die. Since the trust owns the life insurance and not you, it is not subject to estate taxes when you die, as you have no ownership of it any longer.

The reason for doing this instead of giving ownership of the life insurance to someone else is simple. There may not be someone that you trust or want to leave the funds to. This gives you the ability to eliminate risks of ownership or even help you to keep legal control over the policy while you are still alive.

Yet there are some things that you need to consider if you are to make this happen for yourself. First, life insurance trust must be considered irrevocable, as this removes your ownership from the trust. If you own it, you pay tax on it. Second, you cannot name yourself as the trustee of the trust. Finally, you must put this type of trust in place at least three years before you die.

Charitable Remainder Trusts

As mentioned earlier, another option that you have is a Charitable Remainder Trust. In this type of trust, you will make an irrevocable gift of property that is made to a tax free charity. When you set this type of trust in motion, you will receive a set income from the property that you give while you are alive. In doing this you secure a lower estate tax as well as a lower income tax. The only catch is that when you die, the property must go to the charity. This will eventually cost you more to donate the property than the tax benefits that you will receive, but if you want the property to go to charity anyway, it can be a good thing.

Generation Skipping Trust

Earlier we talked about the generation skipping trust and how regulations were put into place to limit the problem of people giving their grandchildren their estate to avoid paying estate taxes on it. But you can set up a generation skipping trust to help manage your funds if you wish.

Usually, this is something only those that have a good amount of wealth will take advantage of. Nevertheless, if you want to leave a trust for your grandchildren, this trust will establish that. Here, the trust only will pay a set income to your children. When your children die, the funds that are left in the trust are given to the final beneficiaries, your grandchildren.

When you die, the property is still included in your estate. That means that if you have more property that puts you over the estate tax threshold, your estate will pay tax on it. But what it does do is help you avoid the second taxing that would happen when the property is passed to your children and then to your grandchildren.

You are limited as to how much you can leave in this type of trust. If you leave more than what is considered the limit for the year in which you die, there will be stiff tax penalties for the amount over it.

Should you consider this type of trust if your children are well off and do not need the property that you will leave? If the property will simply pass to your grandchildren when your children die, this type of trust can limit just how much will be taxed.

Survivorship Deeds

Like other methods described here, a survivorship deed can work in a key manner. When you purchase property, the deed is placed in the name of two people. When one of those two die, the other gains full ownership of the property. You can also change a deed to provide this same benefit. The benefit of doing so is simple. When the first individual on the deed dies, the other inherits the property as an owner and therefore avoids probate or taxation on the property.

This is a good way of avoiding costs on the property twice (such as when both property owners die). Yet it does not work well unless all property is going to one individual when the other dies. For those that want this property to go to several people, this type of deed will not provide for that. It works best for husband and wife situations. To set this type of deed up, talk to your attorney about survivorship deeds and their benefit to your estate plan.

DISCLAIMING GIFTS

Disclaiming gifts may be another way to reduce the amount of taxes that your estate will pay when you die. A disclaimer is not a trust, but works somewhat similarly. A disclaimer is simply an allowance for the beneficiary to simply decline a gift that is given to them, which can include inheritances. When the beneficiary declines the gift, the gift is then passed to the alternative beneficiary.

Why would someone do this? The most common reason for disclaiming gifts is as simple as the funds are not needed by the beneficiary. If you stand to inherit $200,000 and are well off and simply do not need it, you can decline the funds, which would pass down to the alternative beneficiary. This can help with estate taxes because the funds do not go through estate taxing two times (once when the funds are given to the beneficiary and again when the beneficiary dies).

With any and all these methods to reduce the estate tax that will happen to your estate, it is important to establish them with your estate planning attorney who can drastically help you to reduce the risk of something going wrong in the planning. Trusts can be complicated to plan and structure legally.

Case Study: Chris D. Carey

A person should begin thinking about estate planning when they have children or acquire a significant asset, such as a house. The planning process should increase the likelihood that a person will accomplish his or her estate planning goals and save money in the long run. No one can

Case Study: Chris D. Carey

see the future, but those who start planning early will be better situated for whatever comes their way.

Gifting is a simple, often overlooked, tax free way to transfer wealth from one generation to the next. The problem with gifting is that once something has been given away, it is gone. Whether gifting is the right choice for someone depends on his or her financial situation and goals.

Proper planning almost always saves attorney fees and expenses in the future. For instance, if someone dies without a will, his or her property will be distributed pursuant to state law, usually to the closest relatives. Even if that is what the person desired, the administration of the estate will be more expensive and time consuming because the administrator will be required to post bond. In a will, the testator ordinarily specifies that his or her executor be permitted to serve without bond. The cost of the bond alone could exceed what it would have cost to do a little advanced planning.

The worst case is this: Elderly owners of a family farm transferred the land to several children without consulting an accountant or their attorney, believing that they were saving money. Their failure to consult with an estate planning professional cost their children the stepped up basis on death and resulted in a capital gains tax liability that far exceeded the costs of probate and estate tax combined.

Chris D. Carey
Laribee & Hertrick, LLP
325 North Broadway
Medina, Ohio 44256
330-725-0531
Fax: 330-725-0666
cdcarey@laribee-hertrick.com

A COMPREHENSIVE ESTATE PLAN: PUTTING INSURANCE PIECES TOGETHER

Throughout this book, you have learned a good deal about the estate plan and crafting one that puts your life after death into perspective. If nothing else, you will be able to understand what is going to happen to everything you have worked so hard to earn. But we have presented it in bits and pieces, as a foundation. Now it is time to help you craft what we call a "comprehensive estate plan," which will put all the pieces together and finally help you establish the best method for managing what is important to you.

What you should understand is that you have in place a team of individuals that can help you throughout the process: your financial planning attorney, your financial planner, your accountant, and your insurance provider. Each individual should understand what your goals are and who the other players in the game are. In this and subsequent chapters, we will focus on putting together a plan that will work for you on all fronts.

To get started, we need to take a close look at insurance — the one thing that most people believe will save their family from taxes and despair after they die. Read through this chapter and understand the basics. Then, schedule a meeting with your insurance agent to talk about the products you have and those that you need to provide your family with the protection they need. We recommend working closely with an insurance agent, rather than just with the company so that you can talk about your needs with someone that will take the time to understand them. If you do not want to do this, you will need the help of your financial advisor to make sure what you are doing makes financial sense in the long-term.

INSURANCE PROTECTION

Insurance provides protection, something that your entire estate plan should provide. It can help in a number of different situations. There are those that die unexpectedly and that means costly bills, as well as the loss of a wage earner in the family. For those that simply cannot work due to disability, it provides additional protection. In addition, it can help to protect you from lawsuits.

One thing you should never do is purchase more insurance than you need. But you must have a good understanding of what you need to make that decision.

What we need to determine here is what insurance products you need to consider as far as estate planning is concerned. Insurance can help protect your estate from being unexpectedly taken away—for example, if a lawsuit should be filed against you or you find yourself disabled. Insurance can also provide you with protection for those assets that you do not have just yet but will have in your estate later. Finally, it can benefit your assets by adding additional savings to your estate. You will need to understand how these three types of insurance are important to your estate's well-being.

Protecting Current Assets

The first reason to have insurance products is to help protect the assets you have so that you do not lose them. Whatever you currently have that is worth some value to you should be insured. Life happens and assets lose their value all the time due to a variety of situations including lawsuits, disability, car accidents, and so on. If you do not think that you need coverage for these things, you are simply wrong. Not having enough insurance coverage will play a role in your estate's value. Just getting sick or a simple car accident is all it will take.

Many believe that they are protected from this type of loss because they can just file bankruptcy on the claims against them. Again, that means giving up your assets, which limits their value to your family later on. Take inventory of what you have and determine its value. Ultimately, this will play a significant role in the value of your estate through any type of situation.

Protect Future Assets

It may seem strange to tell you that you need insurance to protect what you do not have, but that is a real truth. Here, we are talking about future income insurance. Your insurance agent can work with you to determine just how much this is. But what you need to consider is why you need it.

You should have enough protection through insurance for several key things:

- It should provide enough coverage to pay off whatever you owe on your mortgage.

- It should provide enough coverage for your family for five to ten years of lost income. This means how much you bring home, including overtime and bonuses.

- It should cover large expenses that you foresee, such as your child's college education.

These things are important to note because you want to make sure your family can live the standard of life they are accustomed to without your income. Providing enough coverage can help them make it through while they look for additional ways to make ends meet down the road.

An important note to consider here is that of stocks and mutual funds. If this is part of your estate, you should consider what type of coverage you need for the losses that can happen there as well. If your estate's value is wrapped up in real property, this too should be taken into consideration.

With life insurance, you need to consider the costs that will be necessary to maintain the current standard of living should you or your family lose your income either now or after you die.

Insurance for after You Die

While insurance products can protect your family and help make ends meet, they can also do more. For example, they can help you level off the gift giving that you will do in your estate plan. If you need additional funds to provide for an equal gift to your loved ones, this may need to be included in the insurance products that you have.

If you feel the need to leave behind a substantial amount of money to someone, a life insurance policy can provide it. But it can be costly to do this because of the monthly or yearly insurance premiums that need to be paid. For this reason, work with your insurance agent to determine the policy that will provide you with the most long-term benefits.

TYPES OF INSURANCE COVERAGE

As you know, there are many types of insurance products, each with their own specific benefits to you and to your family. In estate planning, you need to carefully consider each of them.

Here are a few things to think about.

Health Insurance

Health insurance is something that you have not thought about in regard to estate planning. But if you do not have some form of health coverage, chances are good that when you do die there will be expensive medical bills to pay, which could potentially wipe out your estate in the process.

You need health insurance for basic needs such as trips to the doctor's office. Be sure to look closer at what happens when something larger and much more expensive happens. Do you have coverage for such things as long-term care, cancer treatment, hospitalization, and rehabilitation? What does your health coverage provide in these cases?

An important thing to do is look at the maximum amounts on your policy. Some policies have "maximum payment per incident" or "maximum lifetime benefits." These maximum amounts will help define how much your estate can be hit by a large medical bill. For example, if it only covers 70 percent of the medical bills per incident that leaves a potential 30 percent behind that someone has to pay, which would come from your estate. This is a highly expensive bill if, say, you were to suffer a heart attack and needed long-term rehabilitation. In your estate plan, you must take into account the potential for large costs that your health insurance potentially will not cover.

The solution to these costs is not to set aside some funds for them, but to provide yourself with adequate health insurance to cover them. Having 100 percent coverage will provide you (and your family) with peace of mind knowing that if (or possibly when) something happens that the bills are paid in full.

Disability Income Insurance

With disability income insurance, you provide protection in case something happens to you and you are unable to work or earn an income. Many people do not take this type of insurance as seriously as they should, but disability can happen for many reasons.

Unlike life insurance, disability insurance provides you with protection from being unable to earn an income while you are still alive. You can purchase disability coverage if it is not provided to you by your employer, which is often the case. There are two main types to consider.

- **Short-Term:** Short term disability provides you coverage for a period of three months or longer and is provided to you when you use your current or future vacation balance.

- **Long-Term:** In comparison, long-term coverage is provided for a longer length of time, usually for many years, which will replace your income or a large part of it.

When considering the purchase of disability insurance, it is essential to consider what the policy is providing. One thing to consider is what percentage of coverage it provides. Some policies limit this quite substantially. Obviously, you want as much as you can get. Some policies allow you to choose which percentage is right for you.

Another consideration is the "cost of living adjustment." This means that payments will adjust for inflation over the time it is used, a quite important feature. Also, consider how long the disability coverage will pay out. Some policies call it quits when you hit retirement age and begin to receive social security from the federal government.

Disability insurance can help protect your estate, too. It provides you with the means to make money when you otherwise could not. Those that find themselves unable to work and without this type of insurance can lose virtually all that they own due to the costs of living. Protecting your estate means having enough coverage to provide you with an income in any situation.

Long-Term Care Insurance

Catastrophic illness can happen to anyone at any time. Some of the most disturbing and shocking news that we hear is of a completely healthy person being diagnosed with a catastrophic illness that wipes out their future. Long-term medical treatment can be one of the most expensive things a family can face; there is no doubt that you need some method of paying for it. In comes long-term care insurance, which may protect you against this type of medical expense.

Whereas disability coverage protects you from losing your ability to provide income for your family, long-term care insurance provides you with protection from the expenses that go along with the illness or accident you are facing. Since it is nearly impossible for you to determine when and if this happens to you, you have two choices to consider. You can put some money away in your estate plan to pay for long-term care (which may push you over the allowable limit to avoid estate taxes if it is not used) and hope that it is enough or you can invest in long-term care insurance.

Many people end up in assisted living facilities because their spouse and children cannot take care of them on an ongoing basis in their home. You may even dictate in your estate plan what your wishes in these situations are. Nevertheless, entering a nursing home, a long-term assisted living facility, or in home care needs to be paid for.

When planning for long-term care insurance, make sure that it will work with your disability insurance. With your insurance agent, determine what your needs are in terms of the amount of coverage, as well as what may be covered by the disability insurance that you purchase. In addition, determine how well the long-term care insurance works in relation to the health care coverage that you have. You want to make sure that coverage extends throughout your time of need, without any lapses in coverage, which could cost your estate a considerable amount of money.

With the help of your insurance agent, determine the right amount of health care coverage for your needs. Without this type of long-term care insurance or some other method of paying for it, your estate must pay for the cost of your long-term care needs. If there is no method to pay for this, your estate could be drained of value in order to pay for these needs.

Auto Insurance

You did not think we would mention this type of insurance, did you? The fact is that all types of insurance are important to your estate plan including auto insurance. With this type of coverage, there are several key areas to think about. First, you simply should never drive a car that does not have coverage according to your state's laws. A simple traffic accident could cause you thousands of dollars (if not more) in this case.

Second, look at the type of auto insurance policy that you have. The most important consideration is that of "liability" coverage. Does the policy limit you on a per person or per incident basis? If there is a limit in this regard, it could cost you a considerable amount of money.

The best route to take in planning your estate is to sit down and talk with your insurance agent about what types of auto insurance you need, how much you need, and what type of limitations are on the coverage. In most cases, they will help you determine, based on your specific situation, what the needs are. You should always have plenty of auto insurance for all your vehicles. A simple accident can cause hundreds of thousands of dollars in damages, lawsuits, and fines that could put a serious dent in your estate plan.

Homeowner's Insurance

Like auto insurance, homeowner's (and renter's) insurance is a product that you should have. If you have a mortgage, there is no doubt that you have to have homeowner's insurance. The lender will require it. But what if your home is paid in full? Even if you think you can rebuild the entire house on the funds that you have, you should still have homeowner's insurance.

Why do you need it? There is one word that you need to consider: liability. The main reason to have homeowner's insurance is for protection from the loss of your home. Yet it also should provide you with adequate liability coverage. Let us say that someone comes into your home and is hurt when your large television falls on them. Not only will they sue you for injury and medical damages, but what if they can no longer work? What if they win a claim of mental anguish? Here, there is the potential for a serious amount of cost to you and your home. Plenty of people end up losing their home (not to mention other estate property) in the process of these lawsuits. Working with your insurance agent, determine what the worst thing that could happen to you is and plan for it in your estate plan. Enough homeowner's insurance is vitally important here, not just to cover the home itself, but for liability coverage as well.

Umbrella Liability

We just talked about the importance of liability coverage with auto and homeowner's coverage. Yet chances are you do not have enough coverage with those policies. Although this sounds awful, it is a simple fact: The more valuable your estate is, the more likely that someone will go after you for a larger amount of money. It takes one auto accident or one fall on your property to hurt you in terms of your estate's value without the right amount of coverage.

For this reason, many insurance agents suggest using an umbrella policy to provide additional coverage for any type of liability claim against you. This extends further than any other liability that you have, providing you with much more coverage.

Work with your insurance agent to determine the best coverage for you. A good insurance agent can help you determine if you do need umbrella liability coverage, how much, and what is too much. Determine the worst case scenario and work from there.

Life Insurance

We know that you have been waiting for this type of coverage to be mentioned. We have saved it for last for one main reason: It is complex and should be taken very seriously.

Life insurance, when you die, pays a significant amount of money to your beneficiaries. That is the simple truth of what life insurance is. You will find that it gets a bit more complex as we move on. Yet the point of it is to have a life insurance policy in place that will pay someone out when you die for any number of reasons.

Here are some reasons why you need to consider life insurance as part of your estate plan:

1. **It will help replace the income that you bring into the family unit when you die.** Even if you know you will live beyond your income earning years (which there is no way of knowing), this benefit can be immensely important to the family that you leave behind.

2. **It provides liquidity.** That means that when you die the funds are easily accessible. For people who have value that is mostly in real estate or other assets, getting cash to your survivors will be important. Life insurance can provide that.

3. **Estate taxes can be covered.** You can use your life insurance policy to help your survivors pay estate taxes. As we mentioned before, eliminating estate taxes is nearly impossible, but providing funds to cover them is not that difficult when you can use a life insurance policy to do it.

4. **It can pay off the debt that you leave behind.** If you have debt in any form, you can use your life insurance policy to pay them off if and when you die. This removes the requirement that your survivors find the funds to pay off what you owe.

Now, that is a basic look at what life insurance can provide you. But if you have talked to your insurance agent at this point, you also know that there are a handful of different options for you to consider. This is where it can get complex if you do not have a handle on the right insurance product for your needs.

First, determine if you need life insurance. If you need to provide for any of these benefits to your family, you need it. If you do not need to provide these, you may not need it or may not need an extensive policy.

Next, determine what term your life insurance needs to provide. Long-term insurance is important in some cases. But in others term life insurance, which only extends for a time period, may be all that is needed. For example, you may need term life insurance until you are no longer working because at that point, you are not earning an income that needs to be protected anymore. On the other hand, most people carry some debt throughout their life, so long-term life insurance may be necessary to pay this debt off in the event of your untimely death.

Now, let us look at several key types of life insurance and what they can provide to you. Work with your insurance agent to define what you need and what you will benefit from the most.

Whole Life Insurance

For most people, this is the only type of life insurance they know about. Whole life insurance is a straightforward plan. You make premium payments over the time of the insurance product. Part of that payment will go into a special account that earns interest. It develops a cash value over time that can even be borrowed against while you have the insurance in effect. What is more, should you cancel your policy, you get the cash proceeds that are being "saved" for you back.

Universal Life Insurance

Just like whole life insurance, universal life insurance provides you with a guaranteed return on your investment. This type of insurance became popular when interest rates and inflation were high in the 80s, but is still available. The benefit that it provides in contrast to that of whole life is a higher rate of return. Your policy will provide you with details on what specifically it will potentially return to you. Like whole life insurance, it does provide you with a cash value over time.

Variable Life Insurance

With variable life insurance, you take some control over where your money is invested. Some people have more of a risk threshold and want their funds to earn more by putting them in the stock market. Others feel safer with bonds. Yet the potential here to benefit can be high and risky. In some cases, you can lose a considerable amount of money, like when the stock market plummets.

Term Life Insurance

The biggest difference between whole life insurance policies and term life insurance policies is that term products do not have any cash value while you are alive. Not until you die will they pay out. The other difference is that if the policy is no longer in effect, it pays nothing, even when you do die. It is for a specific term or length of time.

Term life insurance is offered by a wide range of insurance companies and there are plenty of different plans to choose from. One that you may encounter is called "annual renewal term policies." With this type of product, your death benefits do not increase, but when you are younger, your premiums are adjusted yearly. Then, you have those policies which "lock" you into a specific premium for a set amount of time, meaning that during that time the premium does not go up or down. Finally, you have those that provide for "decreasing term" insurance. Here, the premium payments will stay the same over the entire policy period, but the death benefits go down as you age.

Company Provided Life Insurance

Your employer may provide you with some or all your life insurance. Many companies offer this type of incentive as a benefit to working there. Yet not all policies are the same. One key thing to do is to talk with your human resource manager about what policies they have for you, what they include, and what they provide. Do not assume that if you have a $250,000 life insurance policy through your job that it is a straight life insurance policy.

One type of insurance product offered through employers is a "key person life insurance policy." This insurance is provided for the highest ranking individuals in the company. If you own a business, you may have this coverage for yourself, too. Another type is called "split dollar life insurance." This type of insurance provides for a more complex situation that is used to provide insurance for several of the company's high ups. If you have this type of policy, it is important to find out from your human resource manager exactly what it is providing you.

For those that do not hold the top positions within a company, which would be most, do not worry — there is likely life insurance available to you through the company. Sometimes, employees do not realize they have it either. What is more, you may have the ability to obtain it in larger amounts if you purchase extra coverage through your company. For some, this type of insurance is limited to only cover your death if you die while working for the company or traveling for the company. Again, you need to find out from your human resource manager what you have and what you can purchase in addition to that.

LIFE INSURANCE AND TAXES

You knew that there was going to be taxes on your life insurance, right? There are, and you need to know what to expect so that you can plan for it in your estate plan. In some cases, those that have the ability to control their life insurance policies find that the value of that policy can be added into the value of their estate, therefore pushing your estate's value higher.

As we mentioned earlier, estate taxes come into play when your estate is valued higher than the allowable limit (the estate tax threshold). Now, before you begin to write off life insurance as part of your estate, consider several things. First, unless you go over the estate tax limit for the year that you die, you will not have to pay any taxes on it. These limits change from year to year, so check with your attorney to determine what this is likely to be in coming years.

The good news is that even if you do go over the allowable amount, there are several key ways that you can avoid taxes on your life insurance. We touched on this in earlier chapters, but let us go into a bit more detail.

If you transfer the ownership of your life insurance policy to someone else, then you no longer own it, and therefore it cannot be considered part of your estate. Unless it is part of your estate, it cannot be taxed when you die. Yet the key here is that once you sign it over to someone else, you lose control of it. You cannot change your beneficiaries, you cannot cancel your policy, and you cannot otherwise manage the policy. Another drawback here is that it can potentially cause you to pay gift taxes or federal estate taxes when you transfer the funds to someone else.

The other option that you have to help you avoid estate taxes for your insurance policy is that of an irrevocable life insurance trust. Here, you will give up control of your life insurance policy, but you do not have to consider the death benefit being included into your estate's value for taxation.

One key element to realize is this: You cannot make changes to your life insurance policy like this (transferring ownership) and see benefits if you die within three years of doing so. The government has limited the transferring of life insurance to avoid estate taxes to three years prior to your death so that you cannot change these terms on your death bed. If you plan to make these changes, do it sooner rather than later.

Check with your financial planning team to make sure that you understand the tax implications that could affect you here. Determine what the best way is to avoid the taxes that you are facing with life insurance. This is a collective effort. Your insurance agent is likely to just sell you as much life insurance as you need. But, with the help of your financial planner, your accountant, and your attorney, you can determine the tax implications on purchasing that level of insurance.

Balance the amount of life insurance that you have with the amount allowable without pushing your estate's value over the threshold, therefore causing it to be taxed. Ultimately, you need to make sure that having too much life insurance does not hurt your estate plan.

TO SUM IT UP

Now that you know what life insurance can and cannot provide you, consider what this means for your needs.

1. If the worst happened to you, what would it do to your family? What type of insurance product do you need to provide coverage for you and your family and to what degree? The worst case scenario should be considered here. Weigh the worst case scenario with the cost of the policies that you are considering.

2. What is at risk? If you do not have enough coverage of any type, what could you and your family lose in the process? In many cases, this may very well be everything that you have, including your home. Determine, with the help of your attorney, what the most is that can be taken from you through the laws of your state.

3. How long do you need the coverage? Some forms of insurance only need to be held for a period of time. Others are needed over the lifetime that you are in possession of them. Determine the right length of coverage per insurance product and adjust it to make the most sense in your life and estate plan.

On a final note, you may want to find out about other protections that are available to you through your state government. For example, some long-term medical coverage can be provided to you through these governmental programs. As we mentioned, your family may need to pay this back as part of the Estate Recovery Act out of your estate when you die.

Insurance is a key factor in your estate plan. For many, it helps to provide for the connection, and ultimately for the funding, of several key aspects of your estate. Whatever you use it for, make sure that you weigh the cost of the insurance, the benefits it provides, and the reward that it will provide to those that you leave behind. For most people, some life insurance and other insurance products are immeasurably beneficial to their financial well being both before and after they die.

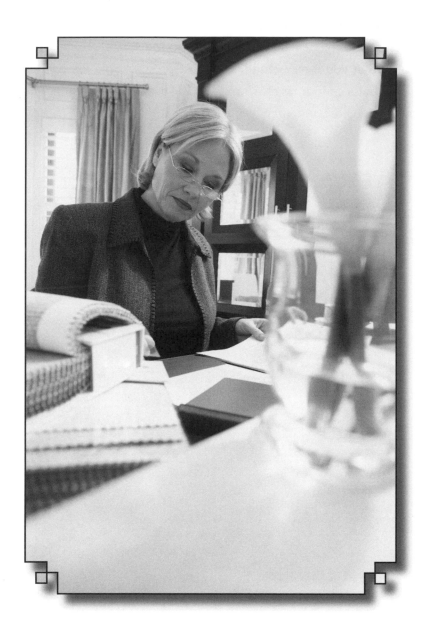

11

PLANNING FOR LONG-TERM CARE

In previous chapters, we have touched on some important topics in relation to planning your estate once you die. It is also important to consider some aspects in your estate plan for before you die. Now that you have a good understanding of the products available to help you throughout the planning of your will, it is important for you to consider the long-term care needs, medical requirements, and financial decisions that must be made. Taking care of much of this will happen with your will, as we have talked about. Yet you need to ultimately define what your wishes are so that they can be carried out in full.

IT WILL NOT HAPPEN TO ME

One of the greatest problems you will have is the mentality that nothing bad can or will happen to you. There is ultimately no way to predict what the future holds and how you will die. While many like to think that they will die quietly, painlessly in their sleep, it is also possible that the long-term, worst case scenario will happen as well. As you age, your body becomes more at risk for both physical and mental challenges. While you are in a good position, you need to make decisions for the "what if" situations that could potentially happen to you.

If you do become mentally challenged in the future, such as with Alzheimer's or another limiting disease or condition, you will not be able to make the right decisions for yourself or your estate. It may fall on whoever is your next in line if you do not make these decisions now. Even if you do pull through from these conditions, in the end it can still hold you at the mercy of those that have been forced to make decisions for you, such as your spouse, your children, or others.

At any age and in any health situation, you should have these basic considerations laid out so that in the untimely situation of your death or illness there is no doubt what your desires are.

To help you do this, let us talk about several key aspects in caring for yourself and your family that you should have written down.

MEDICAL DECISIONS TO CONSIDER

How do you feel about your life being prolonged by a machine? There are two thoughts to this. Some do not want a machine to keep them alive at a potentially high cost without any benefit in the end. For others, the chance that some medical miracle will happen or that they will recover is enough to want this type of treatment used. There are all types of methods that can be used to prolong your life through medical devices and services. Only you know how you feel about these situations.

In recent years, the Supreme Court has ruled that patients have the right to die with dignity. They have the right to not go through painful, overly stressful, and highly expensive treatments that can prolong their life artificially. Every state has also confirmed this right.

Why should you make this decision? The facts are simple. If you do not make this decision, you put it in the hands of those that love you. Will they be in any real condition to make this choice for you? Will they regret the choice that they make years later? Will they question whether they made the right choice for the rest of their lives? If you make the decision, you lessen the needs and the risks placed on your family.

Once you have made the decision about your wishes, which is something that you should talk about with your closest loved ones, you should put it in writing. Each of the states has put in place an allowable, simple document that any person can complete to help determine what these wishes are.

You will need to prepare two types of documents to make your wishes known:

- **Declaration:** This is a statement written down that tells doctors and health care personnel what your specific wishes are regarding various types of treatments. This is also called a "directive" or a "living will." A living will does not leave property or other possessions through it, but spells out your medical wishes to medical personnel.

- **Durable Power of Attorney:** This second document selects one person to be responsible to make sure that your wishes are carried out. This person is also called an "Attorney in Fact." This person can also have a variety of other responsibilities if you wish them to, including:

  ○ The ability to hire or let go medical personnel as needed.

  ○ The ability to have access to your medical records, including all your personal information, usually to help make decisions for you.

  ○ The right to visit you at the facility where you are even when other visiting is restricted.

○ If someone does not honor your wishes, they can get court authorization to make it happen, such as giving or withholding the treatment that you have requested in your living will.

Sometimes, a durable power of attorney is given a specific health care proxy, which is a statement by you giving them the right to make medical decisions for you. As described here, this works the same as an attorney in fact would. A health care proxy is simply another term for this right.

One of the most important things that you need to do here is to determine who the right person will be to have the durable power of attorney over your situation. This person should be someone that is likely to be close enough to your residence so that he or she can quickly make decisions as necessary. Indeed, the person must be willing to provide this for you, which may mean extensive care at the hospital or other situations. He or she should also be someone that you can trust to carry out your decisions and not to be swayed or convinced otherwise. Family and doctors can often try to influence a decision one way or another. Finally, the person must be someone that can understand your medical situation and make decisions based on this information.

Some states have requirements on who can and cannot be your attorney in fact or durable power of attorney. For example, most states do not allow doctors to hold this position. Also, note that as long as you are of sound mind, you can change your decisions anytime that you need or want to.

Finally, you need to decide on what to put in your living will. The good news is that you do not have to be a medical professional to make these decisions, but you should educate yourself on the options that lay in front of you. In your declaration consider making decisions about these things:

- **CPR, cardiopulmonary resuscitation:** Do you want them to try and restart your heart? To what length?

- **Respirators:** Do you want them to keep your body breathing through machines?

- **Surgery:** Do you want them to take any and all means necessary through surgery to improve your situation?

- **Medications:** Do you want medications administered to you to reduce the amount of pain that you are in? Do you want medications that can make you more comfortable in your last hours or days?

- **Feeding Tubes:** Do you want doctors to provide food and water provided to you through artificial means (such as through feeding tubes) when you cannot eat on your own?

- **Blood:** Do you want blood or other blood related products administered to you as needed?

- **Testing:** Do you want all possible tests run on you, such as diagnostic tests?

- **Dialysis:** Do you wish for the doctors to use dialysis on you in critical situations?

- **Drugs and Antibiotics:** Do you want these administered to you when you are in a critical situation?

When you look at these questions, you need to consider them thoroughly. In what circumstances do you want these treatments to be used and when should they not be used? Do you want to lay out what you want here in your declaration or living will or do you want to leave the decisions to your attorney in fact? Of course, for those with long-term disabling conditions, the decisions may be quite different from someone that is relatively healthy that ends up in a critical condition.

When They Go into Effect

It is important for you to understand when your documents will go into effect. In most cases, there are three situations in which this can happen:

1. You are diagnosed with a terminal condition or you are in a permanent state of comatose. Some states also put these into practice for specific illnesses and conditions which you should ask your attorney about.

2. You cannot communicate for some reason about the medical care that you need. This means in situations where you cannot communicate in writing, orally, or through gestures.

3. When medical personnel are told that you have written directives for your medical care, they go into effect. In some cases, this information can be placed in your hospital or other medical records so that they will know what your wishes are from the start of treatment.

You may be able to make your health care documents effective immediately in some states. This may be important for those that find themselves in situations where they are facing long-term illnesses or conditions that affect their mental capacity down the road.

You should work closely with your attorney to establish a living will and durable power of attorney as soon as possible. It can and should become part of your estate. You should notify the person that you want to be your attorney in fact and make sure they agree to make the decisions that you have set forth. Give copies of your living will to several key people to make sure that someone has it when the time comes.

To help you make decisions regarding your life sustaining efforts, use, your regular physician, specialty doctors, and research to help you.

Finalize Your Health Care Decisions

Now that you have your documents created, you need to have them finalized, which is an easy process. Each state has its own special requirements which your attorney can help you with. But you will need to sign your documents, as this will show that you agree to them and that they are your wishes. You will need witnesses or a notary to be present when you do sign them. Those that are present must be able to state that you were of sound mind when making these decisions and that you were over the age of 18.

Give your finalized documents to:

- Your attorney in fact.

- Your doctor with whom you work with regularly or the one that is handling your health situations currently.

- The health care facility that you commonly use, including the hospital you are most likely to be treated at.

- Any other people that are important to you and that should be made aware of your situation and your decisions.

FINAL ARRANGEMENTS

Perhaps one of the most challenging things for people to consider is their own mortality. Yet when you are planning your estate, you should consider the final arrangements that you need and want at the time of your death. You can do this in your estate plan. It can help to ease tensions and stress on your family. It can also help to alleviate the costs of your final arrangements when you plan for them in your estate plan.

The important questions to answer are these:

1. What do you want done with your body when you die?

2. What religious ceremonies and other ceremonies do you want?

Only you can say what you want to happen here. If you leave all these decisions for family members, it is important to realize both the emotional strain and the financial strain that it can cause for you. When you make plans now, you may even be able to make final arrangements more affordably than if they are done at the time of your death.

What should you consider making decisions on? Any and all aspects of your final arrangements should be spelled out for your loved ones in your own wishes. You should consider special instructions, too. Here are a few things to think about:

- Do you want a traditional or religious funeral service? This will usually include the embalming of the body, the resources of a funeral home, and the cremation or burial of your body.

- Do you want a simple funeral service that does not include embalming? Sometimes individuals would rather have a memorial service or even independent arrangements made for them.

- Will you donate your body to a medical school or for other scientific research? If so, you will need to make arrangements for this with the organization you plan to donate to ahead of time. In most cases, once the body has been used for medical study it is then cremated.

- Do you want to donate any livable organs from your body? Giving to an organ bank should be set up beforehand or should be entrusted to your attorney in fact. Once your body has donated these organs, the rest of the body will go to whoever you designate to take it in order to be buried or cremated as you like.

- Do you have other wishes that you would like to express for your funeral, your burial, or the manner in which your body is treated?

As with your medical decision documents, you should have your final arrangements declared in a written statement, with all the same information provided. Do not include this information in your will, as your will is not normally read until well after your funeral will be held. The document that you create must be readily available at the time of your death or even right beforehand.

MAKING FINANCIAL DECISIONS

Just as in the case of medical decisions, you also should spell out your needs and wishes for the financial decisions that must be made. Often people get into a position where they no longer can communicate what their wishes are. When it comes to money there almost always are a number of people trying to get their hands on it, no matter what background they come from.

Just as you have created a set of documents for the medical decisions that you wish, you should do the same for financial decisions that arise when you no longer can make your own wishes known. This involves the use of a durable power of attorney who is someone that you leave your financial needs in the hands of. Again, this person is called your attorney in fact and makes decisions for you based on the wishes that you set forth when you do have the ability to do so. Again, every state in the union recognizes these types of documents.

What if you do not appoint someone to make these decisions for you? In that case and when the situation arises, those that wish to help you make those decisions regarding your finances must get court appointed power of attorney, which may be in your best interest. The procedure to make this happen is called "conservatorship proceedings" and is a long process that can be expensive. Of course, if you simply plan for this outright by creating a durable power of attorney, you forgo this usually complex proceeding from being necessary.

When creating this documentation, you have the same basic abilities as you do when creating a durable power of attorney for your medical decisions (which can be the same person if you so wish). You will appoint the attorney in fact as well as outline the financial decisions that you want him or her to take when you no longer can do so. You can limit this quite a bit or you can allow him or her to make whatever decision seems to be the best in your situation.

As you can tell, a large part of this proceeding will be having a large amount of trust in the person that you are appointing here. You need to know that he or she will do what you have decided, not what he or she believes is beneficial to you. Realize that this person only has the financial say so that you grant him or her in the document, no more and no less. In general, most attorneys in fact have the ability to make standard payments and deposits for you, such as in an effort to keep your household running. Anything beyond this is something that you should spell out in the documentation.

While it is important for you to take into consideration any and all financial situations and the decisions that you want the attorney in fact to make, there is no doubt that you will not be able to predict everything that could possibly happen. In these cases, you will need to know that the person that is behind you as your attorney in fact is someone that you trust to make decisions for you.

What Should You Have Them Do?

In most cases, people that do write up durable power of attorneys for financial decisions will allow them control over much of their finances. Some things that you should think about including are:

- Management of your retirement accounts

- Operation of your small business and business interests

- Use of your assets to make payments for expenses in every day living

- Making payments for your family as needed

- Handling real estate that you own or will own, such as buying and selling it, maintaining it, paying taxes on it, and other property that you own

- Handling the benefits that you receive from such things as social security, governmental programs, military service, pensions, and Medicare

- Investing the funds that you have as you wish them to be invested, such as in stocks and bonds or mutual funds

- Working with your financial institutions

- Paying taxes and filing your yearly taxes

These are just a few of the situations in which you will want to consider having someone make decisions for you. You may have other needs that must be met when it comes to financial matters. Express them simply or through a complex explanation of just what you want done.

Once you have an idea of what you wish to include in these documents, work with your attorney to set up this durable power of attorney in the same manner as your durable power of attorney for medical decisions has been set up. If this is not the same person for both jobs, make sure they can work together when the time comes.

When To Put Them Into Effect

Now that you have defined your needs and your concerns regarding your financial matters, you need to put them into effect. Finalizing the documents is easy to do, just as we described in medical decisions. You will need to have someone watch you sign the documents, which may include a notary if your state dictates it. You should then provide this document to those that should have a copy including your attorney in fact, your attorney, and those that are close to you.

But when will this document go into effect? You can make this decision. You can file the documents to go into effect immediately, such as when you have been diagnosed with a condition that will leave you mentally unable to make these decisions, or you can make them go into effect when your doctor says that you are incapacitated and no longer can make decisions for yourself. If you go this route, which is called a "springing power of attorney," you should realize that your attorney in fact will have to prove that you are incapacitated by getting statements from doctors. Even then, it can be hard for him or her to gain control of your finances.

Another action that you can take is to trust the attorney in fact to only take over your finances when you no longer can do so even though you give him or her immediate control over them. Of course, you should trust him or her when you appoint him or her to this position, otherwise he or she should not be there.

Often, this is a worrisome matter for people, as handing over their financial situation may be risky to them. Therefore, you should make these decisions carefully and only after you have talked to all involved and feel confident in your decisions.

If you have any concerns about what will happen to you when you are unable to make decisions for yourself or you have any worries about what will happen when you die, spell out your wishes in documentation and appoint an attorney in fact to manage these wishes. Virtually anything can be placed in control here to provide you with the ability to make your wishes happen.

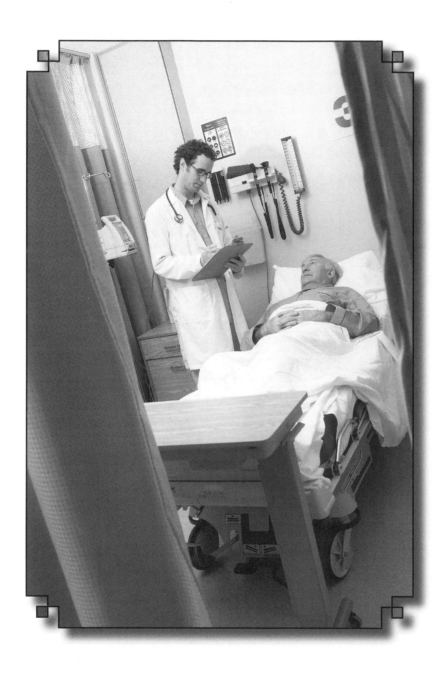

12

YOUR ESTATE PLAN AND YOUR RETIREMENT MONEY

Your estate plan is nearly complete. You have filtered into it where you want all your real property to go. You know how you want the last years of your life to play out. Now you need to factor in anything else that may contribute to the value of your estate or even to those last years. Your retirement income should be considered and planned for in your estate. This will likely take some time to make happen, and it will depend on what goals you have for the funds and what is left over when you die.

INVEST

What tax deferred accounts are there that you can invest in? Before you can have money to plan for your retirement, you have to first put it there. No matter what age you currently are, it is essential to plan for retirement in some form. Here are a few of the tax deferred accounts that you should consider with the help of your financial planner. (Tax deferred simply means that when you invest your dollars this way, taxes are not paid at that time.)

- IRA, Individual Retirement Account

- 401(k) Accounts

- Keogh Plan (which is used for the self-employed)

In these types of accounts, dollars invested into them are not taxed at the time of investment but when the funds come out during retirement. For example, if your employer has a 401(k) account set up for the company, you can invest pre-tax dollars into it through payroll deductions. The funds enter the account and hopefully continue to rise in value, without being levied any taxes, until the funds come out . For this reason, these accounts are called tax deferred. Later, we will explore how each of these can impact your estate plan.

Your financial planner can help you choose the right investments based on your short term and long term goals here.

INTO YOUR ESTATE PLAN

Here, we will talk about planning for any retirement money that you have and how to position it in your estate plan for the most benefit. Retirement money includes funds that you have in an Individual Retirement Account (IRA) or in a 401(k) plan. You may have a pension plan or other plans that have helped you save money for your retirement. Usually, individuals put these funds away so that when they stop working, they have funds to live off of. Yet, as morbid as it sounds, you may not spend it all before you die. That is why you need to figure it into your estate plan.

When you do die, whatever is left over in these accounts is factored in as part of your estate value, which means it could ultimately determine if you pay estate tax or not.

Most people will need to make a single decision about their retirement funds before they move forward. That is, what exactly are you saving the funds in your "retirement" accounts for? Some will use these funds to fund their retirement, meaning that the funds are used for day to day expenses. For others, they use other property to fund their retirement and keep these accounts for their estate for after they die. Let us explore how each of these situations can affect you.

To Pay for Retirement

Let us say that you are using your retirement funds to pay for your retirement years. Here, you are not worried about leaving these funds behind, but using them throughout your retirement years as you need and want to. In this situation, you still have specific goals for what will happen to what is left over, but that is just it: It is only for what is left over.

If you want to use these accounts for this purpose, you need to work closely with your financial advisor to plan for this. They will use a variety of formulas to help to determine exactly what you need in terms of investments to make this happen. They will look at the accounts that you have and their earnings on an annual basis, your current age, and when you plan to retire, as well as the type of lifestyle you want to live during your retirement years.

As part of your estate plan, work with your financial advisor to determine what the best course of action is so that you have the amount of money that you will need to ultimately pay for the type of retirement life style you will live. In doing this, you are not worried about leaving these funds to your beneficiaries.

To Leave Behind in an Estate Plan

For others, and usually most people, retirement accounts are tied to your estate plan. You want to find the right level of living a comfortable retirement but still be able to leave behind funds for your beneficiaries.

When you want your retirement funds to be linked to your estate plan, you will need to work with your financial advisor to make this happen, too. What you will need to do is to link what you are leaving behind to your estate plan. It is no easy job, but one that should be done.

PLANNING FOR YOUR RETIREMENT FUNDS

As part of the process of establishing your estate plan, we have talked about a number of things under the assumption that you want to leave behind property and an estate for your heirs. If you do not want to do this, then you should work with your financial advisor so that you can develop a plan to use up most of your retirement and other estate valued property while you are alive so that little to nothing is left behind. But most people do want to leave something behind and for that, we consider the estate plan.

There are many different things to consider in linking your retirement funds to your estate plan. This includes:

- Your pension

- Your social security benefits

- Your 401(k)

- Your IRA

- Other retirement oriented accounts

Each of these things should be planned for by you in regard to your estate plan, depending on what you have.

Look at some of these retirement accounts and determine which is the right way for you to link them into your estate plan for the maximum benefit.

Pension Accounts

If you have a pension account, which is becoming rarer these days, you need to consider how it ties into your retirement needs. When you do have one, they are likely to be a significant part of your estate planning. There are two things to consider with them. You need to consider a contingency plan, and you need to consider the estate tax implications that they have in regard to lump sum payments.

Contingency Plans

Is your pension insured? If you do not know, you need to find out through your human resource manager. If it is insured, you also need to know how much of it is insured. As many have seen in the last years, many people lose their pensions as a result of a company going under because of a scandal.

You should determine if your pension has coverage through the PBGC, or Pension Benefit Guarantee Corporation, of the federal government. This agency provides some or all protection to some pensions, but not to all. For example, those that have a pension plan through a professional service firm, like a doctor or law firm, are not insured through this agency (if they have under a certain amount of employees). Church pension plans are not insured. Nor are pension plans for a government employee. The only way to know if these plans are insured is to talk with your human resource manager about them.

Along with this information, you need to find out how much it is insured for, as many plans will not be insured to their full value. For some that receive payments before they reach the legal retirement age, these guaranteed amounts of your pension can be lower. If the pension plan includes a survivor or another beneficiary, these can also be lowered as a result. No matter if you have a pension plan insured through PBGC or through your company, the fact is that you need to know all that you can about this plan in regards to how safe it is to count on for your estate plan.

If and when you know how much is guaranteed, you can plan for it. If some or all of it is at risk of being absorbed in the failing of a company, you may want to consider other retirement vehicles to help provide you with the funds that you need during your retirement years.

Payments of Lump Sums Tax Implications

The other consideration is that of tax implications of payments of a lump sum from your pension plan. Some pensions offer a lump sum payment at the time of death (which would forgo the rest of your monthly payments) or at a certain point in the future. Indeed, you will still receive your monthly payments, as these are usually made in addition to those monthly payments. You can find out from your human resource manager if any lump sum payments are likely to affect you.

You need to understand the tax implications as well as the effect that lump sums can have on your estate plan. For most, it means working with your financial planner to determine the right course of action for this situation.

Estate Plan and Your Pension: Here Is What to Look at

There are several key things to take into consideration in regards to your estate plan and how your pension will work with it.

First, consider how well your expenses will be covered by your pension payments during your retirement years. You need to cover your expenses in regard to your housing, food, bills, medical, and health care needs. The goal here is to make sure you have enough to live off of but also to plan for you to leave behind an estate for your heirs down the road. Therefore, you will need to consider if this is your goal or not.

You may want to spend your entire pension on these needs without regard to leaving anything behind from your pension. That means that this is all that you will need to make sure that your pension covers. Other property may be given away over your lifetime or you may leave some behind for beneficiaries.

If your plan allows you to have more than enough in pension income to pay your bills, you can use these extra funds as you see fit. But if your pension plan does not provide for enough funds to cover your living expenses, you may need to consider a plan called a "draw down," which will slowly work into your other assets and then cover your bills in the process of doing so.

If you do have an excess amount, this will then be added to your estate. For some, especially those that live modestly, it could push you into a higher tax bracket for estate tax, and therefore, you should consider the best way to handle these funds to avoid those taxes.

Now, look at your back up plan. You do not have one? What if your pension fails? As we mentioned, pensions are continuously at risk for company failure and corruption, which could put your living expense dollars at risk. For this reason, you do need a back up plan. It could be as simple as drawing from your savings account or other estate holdings to meet living expenses. If you find that you can no longer meet the needs of your estate plan with the reduction of your pension amount, you may need to revisit your estate plan and make adjustments to it to ultimately fix this problem.

Do not forget about inflation either. Many do, and that could mean a serious problem later on. Find out first if your pension plan offers some type of inflation compensation, such as an increase in your pension payment based on inflation. If not, you need to again determine a back up plan.

Social Security

Social Security is a good thing, a bad thing, and a complex thing. As you are still working and earning funds, you hate to see the large deduction from your paycheck that goes to social security. Yet in the back of your mind you wonder if the funds will be available by the time you get there. Depending on where you are in life, this could be a real worry or something that you do not think about.

Nevertheless, it is important to factor social security into your estate plan, as well as what it will provide to you over the course of your retirement years. For many, it becomes the mainstay of these years.

There are several types of social security:

- **Social Security Retirement Payments:** What everyone thinks about is this payment that they will get once they retire at the federal retirement age (which, by the way, changes based on when you were born).

- **Disability Benefits:** If you are hurt or disabled and can no longer work, you may qualify for disability benefits through social security. These can help you make important payments that will safeguard your assets (such as helping to prevent your home from being swiped out from underneath you).

- **Survivor Benefits:** This is a type of benefit that is paid to the surviving family members when you die. A spouse may receive it or a child under 18 may receive it for their deceased parent.

- **Supplemental Security Income:** These are funds that are provided to those that cannot make ends meet in specific circumstances.

Each of these types of social security will factor into your estate plan. Here is a look at how each of them can work for you.

Social Security Retirement Payments

Social Security retirement payments are paid out once you hit your retirement age, based on how much income you have earned over the course of your lifetime. Anyone that has worked in the United States and has paid into the system can begin to collect retirement payments as early as age 62. But full retirement ages depend on when you were born. The federal government is extending this from age 65 (for those born before 1943) to 66 (for those born between 1943 and 1959) to 67 (for those born after 1959.) Social security retirement payments also are dependant on how much you have earned. Depending on that information, you can receive as little as $1,000 per month or up to $2,500 per month. These numbers are adjusted per person.

How does this type of social security factor in to your retirement plan? First, you need to take into account the way that it helps you have the funds that you need for your retirement years. For many, it can provide enough funds, coupled with other funds from pensions and your estate, to help you live a decent retirement. Yet it also should be factored into your estate plan. It should work as money for you to spend during your retirement years that will supplement the other income that you bring in from your estate.

For most people, this gives two options. They can use their social security income to increase the amount of money they have available to them on a monthly basis and simply spend more during that time. Or they can leave more of their assets in their estate plan untouched and use social security for their expenses. This would leave more for your heirs in the long run.

You should be aware, then, that social security payments can play a role in the cost of your estate tax, should there be too much left over when you die.

You can learn from the social security offices exactly when and how much you can draw on your social security by giving them a call or visiting their Web site.

Disability Benefits

Some individuals are eligible for disability benefits from social security if they are injured and no longer can earn an income. This book has revealed how disability insurance works in the insurance chapter, and this type of disability benefit is somewhat the same. The amount of money that you can get through this program depends on how much you have earned and saved into social security.

Disability is not likely to make you rich, as it provides only a modest amount of money that is designed to help you to pay for your expenses while you cannot work. For those that are injured, this type of protection can help save you from having to sell your home to pay for your expenses. If you carry disability until you reach your full retirement age, they simply convert from "disability" into "retirement" payments, although the amount does not change. You can find out how much you would get if you were injured today through the Social Security Administration.

One important note for estate planning reasons: It is recommended that you do not rely solely on the disability benefits that you can obtain. For most people, these benefits are not going to be enough to pay all your expenses, especially if you are injured younger and have had less time to put money into social security. It is highly recommended that you go back and read the information we have provided about disability insurance, which is something that can help you make all ends meet.

Finally, disability benefits will not affect much of your estate plan as the funds are likely to be relatively low.

Survivor Benefits

Survivor benefits are a portion of funds that come from your social security investments. If you die and leave behind a spouse or children, they are likely to be provided with survivor benefits. Sometimes, even divorced spouses will qualify for these benefits.

The amount of money that is gotten through survivor benefits again depends on how much you have put into social security. This amount can be learned by contacting the Social Security Administration. It is likely that this amount will not provide enough funds to maintain your current lifestyle. For most, it does not provide enough help to your family because it is not the same amount as your paycheck.

For this reason, we recommend revisiting our insurance chapter and considering the value of adding life insurance to your estate plan, as this can provide enough funds for your family to maintain the quality of life they are accustomed to and help them avoid losing your home or other assets.

As for your estate plan, determine what your survivor benefits are. Then, determine how that fits into your need for additional life insurance, as well as other benefits that your family will have when you die. In some cases, it will be enough to keep you from needing to purchase a higher life insurance policy. Work with your insurance provider to help you make ends meet.

Supplemental Security Income

Supplement Security Income, which is often shortened to just SSI, is another form of social security, but it is not something you should rely on. Only those that are needy, such as those that have little property, those that are handicapped, or otherwise disabled, will be able to take advantage of this benefit.

The only way that this type of benefit plays into an estate plan is as a last resort. If and when you have lost most of your estate, these benefits may be able to kick in and provide you with the funds that you need. Usually they are unfortunate and tragic events that put you in this position and not something that you plan for.

401(k) and Similar Retirement Plans

Many companies that do not offer pension plans will provide 401(k) plans as their way of helping employees save for their retirement years. They are somewhat like IRA accounts, but a bit different. They usually have a few restrictions on them, and there are different limits.

A 401(k) is usually from a company that is privately held or from one that is publicly traded. 403b and 457 plans are different, as they are for government workers and others that work in tax exempt organizations. You will need to know exactly what type of plan you have so that you can learn its effect on your estate.

Many companies will match the contributions that you make into your 401(k) while others will put in a smaller percentage. Most companies provide from 10 to 20 percent of what you put into your 401(k). You also need to learn how "vested" you are. Some companies limit the funds that can be taken with you if you leave the company (based solely on the amount that the company has matched), which is called your vested value.

The higher this value, the more of the funds that have been matched by your employer factor into your funds.

As implied, a 401(k) is an investment tool that can be taken with you when you leave your employer. You will have a certain amount of time to move those funds into another tax advantages account without having to face penalties on the funds.

When you open a 401(k), you will need to name your beneficiaries. If you are married at that time, this must be your spouse. The spouse can waive these funds if he or she decides it is in the best interests. When you die, your spouse will choose if he or she needs to withdraw the funds from your 401(k) in a lump sum or through payments. Indeed, you will need to determine how much income tax he or she will be charged in these cases. With that said, you should also know that your 401(k) proceeds, when passed to your beneficiary, do not go through probate.

If you have a 401(k), it is important that you work out several key things with your financial planner:

- Determine how much you have in your 401(k) and how it is being invested.

- Determine what advantages you have to this type of plan over others, as well as the disadvantages of having it.

- Determine how much you can invest in your 401(k) for the maximum benefit without running into taxation problems.

- Determine the best payment plan option for you and your family when you begin to draw on those funds during your retirement years.

- Revisit and adjust your 401(k) balances and investments as necessary throughout your life to adjust for risk tolerance.

IRA Accounts

Somewhat more common than the 401(k) are IRA accounts, or Individual Retirement Accounts. IRAs are different plans, though. The laws regarding them are often changed, which is one of the most important reasons you need to work with a financial planner to assess your situation with them. IRAs are tax deductible contributions under special amounts. For example, Congress determines how much you can put into your IRA each year. For the year 2007, you can put in up to $4,000 and for the year 2008, this amount increases to $5,000 per year, which is with inflation indexed increases after this point. For those that are 50 or older, you can put more into your account — termed catch up contributions. It is important to work with your financial planner in regards to your IRA. You need to ensure that you do not invest against your goals for the long-term.

Like any investment, you put money away into an IRA each year. When you retire, the funds are used to pay for your retirement, or you can leave them there as part of your estate. How you plan to use your IRA should help you decide how much you need to have tucked away.

You also need to name your beneficiary for the IRA who will receive the funds from your account if and when you die. Your IRA funds will not go through probate at this time, but your beneficiaries will need to pay taxes on the funds that are given to them. Indeed, you will also need to pay taxes on these dollars when you use them. A Roth IRA is a similar situation, but here you invest dollars after taxing, which would mean that you do not pay them when you withdraw those funds.

Just as you considered these things for your 401(k), it is important to take them into consideration with an IRA:

- Determine how much you have in your IRA and how it is being invested.

- Determine what advantages you have to this type of plan over others, as well as the disadvantages of having it.

- Determine how much you can invest in your IRA for the maximum benefit without running into taxation problems.

- Determine the best payment plan option for you and your family when you begin to draw on those funds during your retirement years.

- Revisit and adjust your IRA balances and investments as necessary throughout your life to adjust for risk tolerance.

It is also important for you to consider the various types of IRAs out there. There are many, each with its own benefits. With the help of your financial planner, you will be able to determine what the right type of IRA is for you. You should compare them, as some have better tax advantages than others.

All these retirement plans allow you to invest in your future. As we have mentioned, it is important for you to consider how you will use those funds, though. For some, the goal is to provide the funds as a way of funding the living expenses, travel, and medical expenses they will incur during retirement years. For others, they are funds tucked away to be placed as part of their state to leave behind to heirs. In any of these situations, realize that your use of the funds is completely up to you. Plan your estate with them kept in mind.

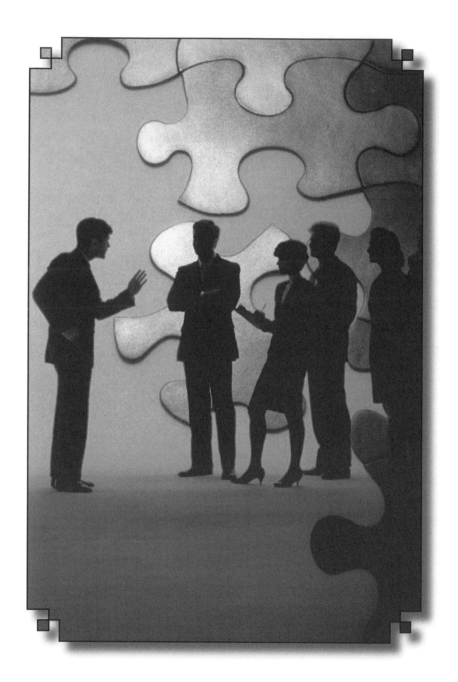

13

WHAT HAPPENS WHEN...?

As you know, life is not simple, neat, or easily organized even with the best laid plans. There are always going to be situations that you cannot plan for because you do not know what will happen. Yet the unique aspect of estate planning is that you can plan for many things "if" they happen. This chapter will address some of the unique situations that often cause people's estate's to get out of line.

CHILDREN AND ESTATES

We have touched on the topic of children in earlier chapters, but let us include some details here that can help you rest assured that your child will be well taken care of. The first consideration for estate planning is what do you mean by children? Different rules need to be considered for those that are children and those that are minors under the age of 18. In each of these situations, different needs must be met.

For minor children, there are two main concerns to consider:

1. Who will take care of your child if you die before they reach 18?

2. How can you provide financial stability to your children if you die before they reach 18? This would include every day living expenses as well as schooling.

Who Will Take Care of Your Child if You Die Before They Are an Adult?

To answer that question, understand that if there is a second parent (one survives the other) this parent would likely have custody of the child. When there is no other parent available, a personal guardian must be established for the child. To document who this person should be, you will need to include it in your will. This is one reason why you need a will no matter what. Yet this person will not become the child's guardian until the court system has deemed it after you die. If for some reason a judge believes that the child should not be with the person you name, he or she has the ability to change this person. This usually only happens when someone contests your will's naming, and even then it is rare, unless he or she can prove that this person simply should not be caring for children.

When choosing someone to care for your child, you must take into consideration his or her willingness and ability. Do not assume he or she will do it, as this is something that should be well thought out. You should also have a secondary person listed in case the first one is unable to take on your children for some reason. In addition, you should name one sole person as their guardian rather than a couple. There are potential problems with naming a couple including who will get the children if that couple splits up.

You can name a guardian for each of your children or one for all them. If you feel that it is necessary to break up your children in order to provide them with the type of relationship that is most fruitful, that is exactly what you can do in your will.

Note that just choosing a guardian is not enough to completely fill in the blanks for that child. What is more, it does not give anyone the right to manage the funds that should be given to this child. We will talk about the financial aspect in just a minute.

What happens when you do not want the other parent of your child to get guardianship if something happens to you? Unfortunately, we cannot provide you with any specific answers for that here. Each case has to be handled on a per case basis. First, you should name whomever you do want to raise them in your will. Second, if the case is not contested by someone, that is who the judge is likely to appoint as your child's guardian. If the case is contested, the only way for the judge to not provide the person with custody of the child is to either determine that the parent is unfit to raise the child based on some information or that the parent has abandoned the child.

The only thing for you to do is to use a letter as part of your will that defines what your concerns are and why you have chosen one person over another. You can explain these decisions in the content of your will as well.

How Can You Provide Financial Stability to Your Children if You Die Before They Reach 18?

The next question that you have to answer is who will manage your child's property until they are old enough to do so. Minors can only own between $2,500 and $5,000 themselves without adult control. This means that you need to appoint someone to manage your child's money. This person will then be called a "trustee," "custodian," or "property guardian." You can also assign someone that will manage your child's property until they reach a specific age, say 21, 25, or even 35.

As we have mentioned throughout this book, there are a variety of ways that you can set up these funds. You can use any of these four methods to leave property behind for your minor child:

1. Custodianship which works under the Uniform Transfers to Minor Act

2. A trust for the child

3. A Family Pot Trust

4. A property guardianship

Uniform Transfers to Minors Act

In all states except for South Carolina and Vermont, you can leave property to your children under this law. The person that is placed in charge of the funds is called the "custodian" and their management of the property ends when the child reaches 18 (or in some cases up to 25 per state law).

In this law, you will document, either through your will or through your living will, what property should be given to your minor child. You name the person that will act as custodian as well as a successor, in cases where the first custodian cannot perform his duties. You finally note that you want the property managed "under the state's Uniform Transfers to Minors Act." This gives this person the ability to collect, hold, invest, reinvest, and manage the property as he sees fit. He or she must keep detailed records for tax records to be filed but does not need to file a separate return. The custodian is allowed a reasonable compensation for managing these funds. The court does not monitor these situations.

Trusts for Children

There are two types of trusts that can be set up to manage your child's funds: a "Child's Trust" or a "Family Pot Trust." The difference is that in a child's trust you leave specific property to a specific child, whereas with a Family Pot Trust all the property is left to all children and can then be used in any amount by each of the children.

With any trust, a person is placed in charge of the property. The documents that establish the trust define what the trustee's responsibilities and rights are. You can establish this trust with a living trust or with a will. When you use a living trust to do this, you forgo any probate costs that could be used otherwise.

The property in the trust is managed by the trustee until the beneficiaries, in this case your children, reach the age at which you have deemed that they will get what is in the trust. You can name this age yourself, but you should consider why you need it to last for such a long time, such as beyond the age of 30 to 35. If the child will not be able to mentally handle the property, it is also possible to set up a special needs trust to care for them with these funds but without giving them control of them. In most cases, the property is managed by the trustee for uses in education, medical necessities, and living expenses.

So which type of trust should you consider? Determine what your ultimate goals are. When children are younger, a Family Pot Trust can be better used to serve the children's needs as a whole. When children are older or when there is a large gap in their ages, a child's trust can allow for the property to be more evenly distributed to each of the children.

Property Guardian

This is a rare and often not a good decision to be made. For example, when you leave property to your children to be managed by a property guardian, the property must go through probate, which means taxes. In addition, property guardians are often required to report for court reviews and face strict, limiting abilities on how they can use the funds. You also have no ability to extend the property guardian's abilities beyond the age of 18. Indeed, it is costly with the fees for attorneys and does nothing to provide you with any idea that the property guardian will do a good job with the children's property.

If you will be using this type of arrangement, it will work for those that have minor children that will be earning a substantial amount of money after you die or they will receive a large gift or inheritance that does not name its own property manager. There are other situations when it can be beneficial, but you must carefully consider these.

Compare the various ways in which you can leave property to your child after you die. Which one provides you with the best outcome for your situation? Work with your financial planning attorney to help you to plan for the right method.

Your Child's Education

Saving for your child's education is an important consideration for anyone and it should be part of your estate plan. Tax saving education investment plans are offered in two different types. 529 Plans and Coverdell Accounts are the two options. Each one should be carefully considered for their benefits and disadvantages.

529 Plans

A 529 Plan is a tax free investment that you can make to pay for higher education expenses to the person that you name as the beneficiary. This person has to be a family member and does allow for you to include this type of fund for any of your children or other family relations that are young. Because you can contribute to the 529 Plan without having to pay taxes and no income tax is assessed on the money that ends up coming from this fund, it is an ideal tax situation to be in. The funds must be used for qualified expenses which are tuition, books, fees, supplies, and other aspects for college, graduate school, or other institutions.

You can contribute up to $12,000 per year to each of these plans. A couple can give up to $24,000 per year. Anything over this and you will be facing a federal gift tax penalty. If you contribute up to $60,000 in one year and do not make future contributions for the next five years, this can help you to avoid the penalty, but you must live this long as well. If funds are withdrawn for any other purpose, the funds are subject to taxes.

These plans are based on state law rather than on federal law, and therefore, you can only use them if the plan is state authorized. Every state has some type of 529 Plan for you to take advantage of. Management companies are in place to manage these based on who the state has chosen to do so. In many states, anyone can contribute to these funds for the beneficiary, allowing grandparents, aunts, and uncles able to do so.

You should understand that these plans are securities of various types, including stocks and bonds. Some states have far more aggressive plans than others. You need to select the right 529 Plan for your situation. Your financial planner can help you consider this need.

There are some things that could be potential drawbacks of this plan. There are highly expensive fees for these plans for the management companies. This can be higher than two percent annually. You should understand what these fees are before you agree to the plan. Also, look into the disclosure policies that the company uses so that you can find out what is going on with your money.

Take the time to learn what types of plans are available to you and what stipulations are in place regarding them. Each state has a different 529 Plan, making it hard for you to learn what the plan offers unless you talk to your financial planner. The other drawback of these plans is that they offer limited investment tools. It is often necessary for you to determine if you are okay with having just a handful of securities to invest in or if you want a broader range of investment opportunities. Of course, no matter which plan you select, there is no guarantee that they will deliver any investment benefit to you.

Coverdell Accounts

Once called Educational IRAs, these accounts allow you to contribute up to $2,000 per year per person investing in a beneficiary's account. These contributions are not tax deductible at the time they are made, but the account is not taxed when it grows, and there is no tax assessed when the withdrawals (for qualified expenses) are taken.

The benefit with this type of educational investment tool is that you get a larger range of investment choices, which means that you can handle the investments more so than with a 529 Plan.

The largest drawback is the limited amount that can be contributed per year to these funds, but they work well for those that have young children. Grandparents or others can also invest in these as an additional investment.

These educational and other methods of taking care of your child, when you cannot do so, are important to consider as part of your estate. Are there other concerns that you have, such as caring for children that are not biologically yours? Perhaps you would like to disinherit a child? These things also can be worked into your estate plan, but with the help of your attorney per specific situation. Handling these on a per case basis is important.

WHAT HAPPENS WITH DIVORCE

Another situation that is often tricky to plan for is divorce. If you are going through a divorce, or do in the future, it is important to think about your estate plan in the process. It is not something that is planned for, but if and when it happens, you need to consider how it will affect your estate plan. There are several key things that need to be taken into consideration, including what will happen to your property and children if you do nothing or what options you have.

In situations like these, you need a specialized attorney, one that has experience in divorce and in estate planning, as the two can be rather tricky to plan.

There is more to settling a divorce than just looking at the property that you have in the here and now. You also need to take into consideration the property in your estate and its future there. You both have an estate plan for what will happen when you die, which may include a number of different people from both sides of the family. Yet when you do divorce, you may not want to have these people in the same situations. In most cases, your estate is split 50/50, which means that the property in your estate has changed.

Although to this point you are considering your estate as "our property," it is important to define it as "my property and your property." During your marriage, you both made purchases that were solely in one person's name. Yet during a divorce, all property that is purchased during the marriage falls under "marital property" now. The bottom line is that you need to inventory what comes to you after the divorce and reassess your estate plan now that it has changed.

So what should you do?

- Overhaul your estate and gift tax marital deductions.

- Redo your will to include a more accurate picture of your life.

- Determine who should get property when you die, including property that you left to your ex-spouse.

- Determine your child's situation in regards to the estate now, which should also include step children, if applicable.

You can still leave property to your spouse if you decide to do that.

The best course of action during a divorce, and afterward, is to determine what property you still have and to arrange your estate plan accordingly. Children can be provided for just as you would before, depending on one or both of your new estate plans. Work closely with your attorney to make these changes in your estate plan as soon as possible after the divorce.

14

PUTTING IT ALL TOGETHER

Putting together your estate plan seems like a huge task, one that involves various elements and can, in short, easily overwhelm someone from the start. Yet that is why we have helped you see the importance of hiring several key people to help you through the process. The first thing you need to do is look at your estate planning team, making sure that they have the skill and the experience and that you can trust them.

But then what do you do? At this point, you should have a basic understanding of what goes into an estate plan and what you would like to include in yours. Hopefully we have opened your eyes to a few situations where you can easily craft your wishes and even avoid costly taxes in the process. Let us organize those thoughts here to get you started in the actual planning of your estate.

STEP 1: WHY ARE YOU PLANNING?

The biggest reason to put together a comprehensive estate plan is as simple as being able to control what happens to your property after you die. But even if you do not care what happens to it (which is not the case most of the time), you still need to consider what will happen to your heirs if you do not plan anything.

Chances are good that they will contribute to the tax system with some high costs on probate and estate taxes coming from your property. If you have any real property that is valuable, there may be a fight, a family problem, or even the loss of that property in an effort to choose where it goes. There is little doubt that in the end, an estate can rip a family apart with the "I should get this" and "you do not deserve anything" problems that most families deal with.

You may have your own reason for planning your estate. Perhaps you want to make sure someone does not get something or you want specific pieces of your estate to go to a certain person. You may just want to make sure that the government does not get too much of your property in the taxes that end up being paid from it.

The point is that you should define why you want to plan your estate so that you can make sure that in the end, your estate plan reflects this desire.

STEP 2: WHAT DO I WANT TO COVER?

Every person's life is unique and with that comes a variety of struggles with what happens in the estate that they plan. Nevertheless, you need to sit down and ask yourself what you need to do in your estate plan. Set forth a few goals that can help to dictate what happens. For many people, this means determining where large assets go and who gets what. The best way to do this is to simply look at the situation from all points of view.

For example, if you have two children and want them each to get a fair share in your estate, how will you make that happen? Perhaps you could have the family home sold and each will get a share of it. However, if you know that your daughter would love to keep the family home in the family, perhaps a life insurance policy for the value of the home could be made up to fund the same dollar value to your son. Look at all options available to you in planning your estate.

If your goal is to minimize the amount of taxes that go to the government when you die, there are likely to be plenty of ways to do this, if you work on it before you die. As you read in our estate tax section, there is little doubt that you can minimize this number, but often much of this has to be done ahead of time.

The question then to ask is, what do you want your estate plan to encompass?

STEP 3: WHO WILL YOU TAKE CARE OF?

Defining who will benefit from your estate plan is an important and often worrisome situation. While you would love to leave something to each of your family members, it is likely that you want to make sure that certain people are taken care of in your estate plan. Of course, you also need to think of yourself in the process. How will you plan for your retirement years?

Consider the people that you want to take care of in your will:

- How will you care for your spouse?

- How will you care for your children?

- Are there step children, adopted children, or other family members that you want to care for?

- Do you plan to leave most of your property for your children or perhaps your grandchildren?

- Are there charities that you want to support?

- How will you care for yourself during your retirement years?

- What type of allotment do you need to make for health care, including long-term care and expensive medical treatments for worst case scenarios?

- Are there others that you want to take care of through your will? If so, how will you do that?

It is important to consider the importance of each of these people. For example, while your second cousin may be someone you want to leave something to, you want to make sure that your children have the funds necessary for their college education first. Take the time to list those that you want to include in your will by importance and the needs that each one has.

STEP 4: CARING FOR YOUR CHILDREN

Although we touched on it in the previous step, often it takes time to consider what needs to be done to care for children. Depending on when you are crafting your estate plan, you may have minor children to plan for. In that case, you need to be concerned with such things as your child's custody, your child's property that you plan to leave them, as well as the educational needs of that child. Even if you do not die, you want to plan for their college education and your estate should be how you do that.

There are many methods that can help you accomplish these goals. We have talked about the process of selecting guardianship, how to establish trusts for your child, and even how to establish educational products to protect their college education.

Yet minor children are not the only ones that should be taken care of. You will want to address the needs of adult children, too and how you will provide for them when you are no longer able to be there.

STEP 5: WHERE ARE YOU AT?

With an understanding of what you want to accomplish in your estate plan, the next step involves simply determining where you are right now. We dedicated several pages to helping you determine your current estate's value. That is a place to start. You also want to consider what you need to accomplish your goals. While everyone wants to leave behind millions of dollars, be sensible in developing a plan that provides for what you realistically can accomplish in your lifetime.

There are two things to consider here:

1. What do you currently own that should be included in your estate?

2. What do you want to earn or add to your value in order to accomplish your estate planning goals?

The person to help you answer question number two is your financial planner, who can help you determine how you will accomplish all your financial goals throughout your lifetime so that when you die, your estate plan is where you want it to be.

As you plan your estate, you should first plan for what you currently have so that ultimately your estate plan only includes what you have, not what you expect to have. But as life progresses, you will need to go back and make changes as necessary.

STEP 6: WHO IS YOUR TEAM?

Keep in mind in the first chapters of this book we talked about the wide range of people that were on your estate planning team. Now is the time to assemble them and to develop a plan with each one of them. Your estate planning attorney, your financial planner, your accountant, and your insurance agent are valuable to you during this time. But do not make the mistake of thinking that anyone can play these roles.

You need to make sure that:

- Your team has experience in estate planning. They must be competent in this particular field to serve you.

- Your team should have proven success and plenty of references for you to check out.

- Your team should be people (not companies necessarily, but real people) that you trust whole-heartedly with your financial future and your heir's property.

Spending some time finding people that can help you with these goals is important. You need an insurance agent, for example, that will tell you how much insurance you need, not how much he or she can convince you that you need. You need a financial planner that is not working for the investments that he or she is pushing. You want to know that he or she has your back throughout this process.

Once you have assembled your team, take the information that you have gathered from Steps 1 through 5 and talk to them about it. Ask them to help you develop plans to make your goals come to life. Going in educated gives you the advantage here. You have plenty of ideas on how to make all your goals happen anyway.

STEP 7: WHO SHOULD YOU TELL?

Even if you have an estate plan in place, you should still make an effort to provide your family with all the information and plans you are making. How many times have you heard stories of families that are torn apart because one child got more than the other in their parent's estate? Even worse, many do not understand what is left over and the value of those aspects to the actual parent. You may have a high value in a simple charm that you are passing down to your grandchild, but the one that gets the car may seem to have gotten more.

The fact is that you need to make sure everyone in your estate plan (and even those you have intentionally left out) knows what to expect. Of course, you do not have to do this. You can die being the only one that even knows that the estate plan is in effect (hopefully your spouse knows).

In addition to these people, you will want to make sure that your trusted friends and family know that you do have an estate plan so that they can help to make sure it comes to life in the event that your will cannot be found.

As you make changes to your estate plan, make sure that you update those that you have included in your estate plan. Otherwise, this can cause a number of problems later.

STEP 8: DID YOU GET EVERYTHING?

It is important to review several things as you develop them. As you develop your estate plan, it can become easy for you to forget certain situations and even find yourself struggling with the specifics of each.

Here are a few things that you do not want to forget (which are commonly forgotten by others):

- Include a residuary clause which will provide for whatever is left over in your estate. Anything that you do not specifically mention in your will should have a destination to go to so that there is no problem.

- Include contingent beneficiaries into your will who will take over for those that cannot inherit what you provide. For example, if someone you list as a beneficiary dies before you do and you do not change your will, the contingent beneficiary gets whatever the beneficiary would have.

- Is your personal representative still someone that you trust to handle your situation? As your life changes, this person may change, too. Look at all situations where you list beneficiaries and guardians to determine if changes should be made there.

- Make sure that your will is properly legalized, as well as any trusts, insurance policies or other estate plans. Notaries are the best place for witnesses, as they do not have anything to do with you; therefore, they are not in any way benefiting from what you are signing.

- Do not rush it. Estate planning does take time, and you do need to plan your will and estate based on a lifetime, in many cases. Take the time to go through all aspects of your will so that you can make sure that ultimately the best plans are laid for your future and your property after you die.

Working with skilled professionals in developing your estate plan should minimize the problems that you face, of course. Nevertheless, no one, no matter how much they can be trusted, is behind your goals as much as you are. Therefore, do your own checking to make sure that your will and estate plan are what you want them to be.

STEP 9: REVISIT YOUR ESTATE PLAN YEARLY OR MORE

Even once you have your estate plan in order, you still need to go back to it and look at it a bit closer each year. Life changes and it changes often. You should even try to have your attorney book a time slot for you each year about the same time (say around your birthday) to come in and find out if anything in your estate plan needs to be readjusted. As your property grows in value, it may be necessary to reassess its effect on the estate plan.

Also, any time that you make serious changes to your estate, such as purchasing real estate, selling real estate, or other significant changes happen, revisit your estate plan to make changes as necessary. If you sell a home that was supposed to go to your daughter because you needed the funds to support your retirement years, you first need to remove it from your estate plan. You may also want to go back to the estate plan to readjust it to now give your daughter a share of the other home that you own so that she and her brother get an even share.

As part of revisiting your will, it will become important to consider the facts and how they relate to your estate tax situation, too. You may find yourself just over the estate tax threshold and therefore need to make adjustments to minimize that level of estate taxable property.

STEP 10: WORK TO ACCOMPLISH YOUR GOALS

Even after you have succeeded in developing your estate plan, you will have to work on them to accomplish your goals. The good news is that there are plenty of ways for you to put together an estate plan that is effective in what it does based on what you currently have. But for those that need to add more value to their estate, you need to do just that.

It is important to consider the importance of your estate plan in relation to your life, too. Life changes, and you may simply change your mind about certain considerations. When that happens, make changes to your estate plan to reflect this.

CONCLUSION

You have successfully planned your estate, right? There is no doubt that you will need the help of a skilled team of professionals to help you accomplish the goals that you have in regards to your estate plan. There is no doubt that virtually anything that you want to accomplish in your will and estate plan can be accomplished. But it is important for you to remain vigilant about making it happen.

Work through this book to help you see what options you have for overcoming the various obstacles that often get in the way during planning an estate. Indeed, if you learned anything, it is the fact that it is essential to plan your estate in some form so that when you are no longer around to make decisions, what you want to happen, happens.

With carefully planning your estate, you can accomplish all your goals from leaving property for your heirs to caring for your minor children and even making sure that your favorite charities are taken care of. Even if you just want to make sure that your estate pays as little tax as it can, that in itself is a reason to plan your estate.

No one wants to think about their death, but everyone needs to consider what will happen to their life's work after they are no longer here or risk it all.

_____ ☙ ❧ _____

APPENDIX

_____

The following pages provide you with samples of various wills and legal papers involved in planning your estate. Since state laws vary, be sure to consult with your attorney before relying solely on the examples.

LIVING WILL

This declaration was made this _____day of _____, 20_____.

I, _____, of my own volition, hereby make known my wish that my life not be prolonged by the use of any machines under the circumstances which I have included below.

If I become terminally ill and my doctor and another consulting physician have concluded that it is medically improbable that I will recover, I hereby declare that no life-prolonging measures shall be taken or shall be stopped when it is clear such measures will only prolong the process of dying. I wish to die naturally, only taking those medications that will make me comfortable.

This declaration shall be honored by my family and my doctor, as it is the final expression of my legal rights to refuse treatment and to accept the consequences of that refusal.

If it has been determined that I am unable to express my wishes regarding the withdrawal of life-sustaining measures, I hereby designate _____as my surrogate to carry out my wishes as stated in this declaration.

(Print the name, address, and telephone number of your surrogate)

Name: _____

Address: _____

Zip Code: _____

Phone: _____

If my appointed surrogate does not wish or for some reason cannot act on my behalf, I hereby designate _____ as my alternate surrogate who will carry out the provisions of this declaration.

(Print name, address, and telephone number of your alternate surrogate)

Name: _____

Address: _____

Zip Code:_____

Phone: _____

Additional Instructions:

(Add any personal instructions here if you so wish)

_____

_____

_____

I understand the contents and consequences of this declaration, and I am emotionally and mentally able to make this declaration.

Signed:_____ Date: _____

(Two witnesses must sign their names and print their addresses)

Witness #1

Signed:_____

Address: _____

Witness #2

Signed: _____

Address:_____

DESIGNATION OF HEALTH CARE SURROGATE

Name: _____

        Last   First   Middle Initial

If it has been determined that I am unable to make informed decisions regarding my medical treatment and procedures, I hereby designate _____ as my surrogate for health care decisions.

(Print the name, home address, and telephone number of your surrogate)

Name: _____

Address: _____

Zip Code: _____

Phone: _____

If for some reason my surrogate does not wish to or cannot act in my best interest, I hereby designate_____ as my alternate surrogate.

(Print the name, address, and telephone number of your alternate surrogate)

Name: _____

Address: _____

Zip Code: _____

Phone: _____

I completely understand that this declaration allows my surrogate to make health care decisions for me, to search for public benefits to defray health care costs, and to approve my admission to or transfer from a health care facility.

(Add any personal instructions here if you so wish)

_____

_____

_____

_____

Additional Instructions:

I also confirm that this declaration is not being made as a condition of treatment or admission to a health care facility. I will inform and send a copy of this document to _____ and _____ so they are aware who my surrogate is.

(Print the names and addresses of two people you want to keep copies of this document)

Name:_____

Address: _____

Name: _____

Address:_____

(Sign and date the document)

Signed: _____ Date: _____

(Two witnesses must sign their names and print their addresses)

Witness #1

Signed: _____

Address:_____

Witness #2

Signed: _____

Address:_____

POWER OF ATTORNEY

This is a warning to the person executing this document:

This is an important legal document which is authorized by the laws of this state. The powers designated in this document are extensive and comprehensive. They are defined in _____ (state laws) of the _____ (your state) laws.

Using this form is voluntary and _____ (state laws) allows the use of any other form of power of attorney if both parties involved agree.

I, _____ (name and address) hereby designate _____ (name and address) my attorney-in-fact.

First: In my name, act in any way that I myself would if I were actually present, with regard to the following matters:

(Here, strike out and initial any of the subdivisions that you do not want to give your attorney-in-fact authority for. If any of the subdivisions are eliminated, this automatically eliminates Subdivision J.)

You must cross out the subdivision and initial it.

(A) Real Estate Transactions

(B) Chattel and Goods Transactions

(C) Bond, Share, and Commodity Transactions

(D) Banking Transactions

(E) Business Operating Transactions

(F) Insurance Transactions

(G) Claims and Litigations

(H) Benefits from Military Service

(I) Reports, Records, and Statements

(J) All Other Matters

(You may include special directives here, but only if they conform to your state's power of attorney requirements.)

Second: This power of attorney will:

(A) Be of indefinite duration

(B) End on _____ (date), unless otherwise ended

Third: This confirms all that the attorney-in-fact should do.

I hereby witness and sign my name on this _____ day of _____, 20_____.

Name:_____

Acknowledgment: Let it be known that this designation will not by affected by the ineptitude of the recipient.

I hereby witness and sign my name on this _____ day of _____ 20 _____.

Name:_____

Acknowledgment: This document shall by recorded or filed by the two clerk or recorder of deeds.

CONSIDERATIONS IN PLANNING YOUR ESTATE

❦ Personal Information: ❧

Name:_____

Social Security Number: _____

Are You a U.S. Citizen: ☐ Yes   ☐ No

Current Address: _____

Phone Number: _____

E-mail: _____

❦ Marital Status ❧

☐ Single, never married   ☐ Married Once (Spouse still alive)

☐ Window/Widower   ☐ Presently Married (Had prior marriage)

☐ Divorced

(If Married) Name of Spouse: _____

Spouse's Social Security Number: _____

Is Spouse a U.S. Citizen: ☐ Yes   ☐ No

❦ Children ❧

How many children do you have (including stepchildren and adopted children)? _____

If you have stepchildren or adopted children, do you wish to treat them the same as your biological children? ☐ Yes ☐ No

Is any child a minor? ☐ Yes ☐ No

⬥ Value of Estate ⬥

The value of your estate determines which the appropriate will for you. Your estate value includes the value of all the property owned in your name, and if married, the value of property in your spouse's name. If any value has a debt, be sure to include that value. Also, list the value of any life insurance policies that you may have. Please note that your life insurance usually does not pass according to your will but it will be distributed to the beneficiaries that you have listed on the policy.

Approximate value of your estate (not including life insurance):
$ _____

Approximate value of your spouse's estate (not including life insurance):
$ _____

Value of life insurance (self and spouse):
$ _____

Total value of combined estates including life insurance:
$ _____

Please note that if you think the value of your estate is over $1 million, it may incur estate taxes. Also note that advanced planning can help you decrease your estate tax.

⬥ Family Farms & Family Businesses ⬥

Do you have a family farm? ☐ Yes ☐ No

Do you have a family business? ☐ Yes ☐ No

❦ Real Estate ❧

Usually, a husband and wife own real estate together and have right of suvivorship. Please note that if you and your spouse jointly own your real estate that your will will not affect how your ownership will pass when you die.

Do you own real estate jointly with your spouse?

☐ Yes   ☐ No

Do you own real estate other than jointly with your spouse?

☐ Yes   ☐ No

If yes, how do you wish to allot your property?

☐ All to spouse

☐ To pass with the rest of estate

☐ My home to my spouse and the rest of my real estate to pass with the rest of my estate

☐ My home to my spouse as long as my spouse lives. Then, my home and the rest of my real estate to pass with the rest of my estate

☐ Different properties to different beneficiaries (please list below each property and to whom you are leaving it and what that person's relationship is to you)

_____

_____

_____

———————℘ Personal Items & Tangible Property ℜ———————

How do you wish to give your personal items? Please be sure to attach a detailed list of all personal items and note which item is to pass to various individuals if you wish to divide your estate as such.

- ☐ All to spouse

- ☐ Specific items to specific individuals, with items not listed to go to my spouse

- ☐ Specific items to go to specific individuals, with items not listed to pass with the rest of my estate

- ☐ Everything to pass with rest of my estate

- ☐ Other (explain below)

_____

_____

_____

———————℘ Specific Bequests ℜ———————

Please note that while you may give specific gifts of cash, real estate, and/ or personal property to individual people or charities in your will, these bequests will be allotted first, which may greatly deplete the value of your estate. If certain listed items cannot be found at your death, then probate of your estate may be complicated. Thus, you should only make bequests of property or cash that you will be sure that you will have when you die. If you choose not to make specific bequests, all of your estate property will pass to your indicated primary beneficiaries. Please note that many states require you to make a "personal memorandum" in which you can make individual bequests separate from your will. However, while these gifts are not always legally binding in most states, your executor will give as much credit to these gifts as your state law allows.

Do you wish to make any specific bequest(s) in your will?

☐ Yes   ☐ No

_____

_____

_____

_____ ℘ **Residuary Estate** ℘ _____

This includes whatever property is left over after paying for all your incurred debts, specific bequests, and the expense of administration. This is typically the property left to your beneficiaries, as many people do not make specific bequests.

To whom do you want to leave your residuary estate?

☐ All to my spouse if he/she survives me and if not, then to my children

☐ A minimum bequest to my spouse, disinheriting him/her to the fullest extent of the law, with the remainder of my estate to be distributed to other person(s)

☐ All to one specific beneficiary other than my spouse

☐ To more than one beneficiary

If you have more than one beneficiary, are they:

☐ Specific people who are to share equally

☐ A group of people described as a class to share equally (ie: my sisters)

☐ Some other unequal division between the beneficiaries (ie: 75% to one beneficiary and 25% to the other)

☐ Other (please explain below):

_____

_____

_____

If any of your beneficiaries is a minor, at what age would you like for them to receive their gift?

☐ 18

☐ 21

☐ Other age (please indicate below)

_____

Please note that if you decide to select an age older than 21, the specific request will likely require a trust. A trust may cause your estate to have additional expenses for the future administration of the trust, which would lower the amount available for your beneficiaries.

_____ ℘ Executor ℧ _____

Your executor, or personal representative, is appointed to ensure that your estate is settled when you die. This process will typically involve going through probate, which is a court-administered procedure that is designed to settle an estate as provided in your will or by the state law. The process of probate involves petitioning a court for letters of appointment, settling creditor claims, finding and distributing assets, and filing any necessary tax returns. While any adult may serve as your executor, some states would prefer you to have an executor that is a legal resident of the state where the probate will occur.

Whom do you wish to serve as your executor?

☐ Spouse

☐ My spouse and a co-executor

☐ My spouse and a successor executor

☐ One executor other than my spouse

☐ Two co-executors, neither of whom are my spouse*

☐ One executor and a successor executor, neither of whom are my spouse.**

*Usually, this option is not recommended because conflicts often arise between the executors, which will complicate the administration of your estate.

**The successor will act only if your first choice cannot be the executor.

If you wish for someone other than your spouse to be your executor, please list that person(s) below:

_____

_____

_____

℘ Guardian ℘

If you have children who are minors when you die and their other natural parent is not alive or cannot become their guardian, the court will typically appoint the person that you name in your will to serve as your children's legal guardian until they reach the legal age of 18. If you are divorced, the court will typically grant custody of your children to the child's natural parent even if you state otherwise in your will. However, be sure to name a guardian in the case that child's other natural parent dies before you.

Do you wish to appoint:

☐ One guardian for my child

☐ One guardian and a successor guardian

☐ Two co-guardians

☐ No guardian

Please list the name, relationship, and address of the person that you wish to appoint guardianship.

1st Choice: _____

2nd Choice: _____

3rd Choice: _____

_____ ℘ Trusts ℞ _____

You can set up a trust to skip giving your estate directly to your beneficiary. With a trust, you can give your estate to a trustee for the benefit of your beneficiary until he or she reaches the age of your designation, such as 20, 25, 30, etc.). Under the directions that you outline in the trust, the trustee will manage your estate under court supervision. While the primary purpose of the trustee is to safeguard the inheritance, the inheritance can also be used for your beneficiary's health, education, or welfare at the trustee's discretion. You also have the option to create a trust to pool your estate, which means that your estate will remain in a single trust until all beneficiaries reach the age of your designation. Here, the trustee still has the ability to apply funds to each beneficiary as he or she has a need, which may lead to not all beneficiaries receiving the same amount of funds. This type of trust could be useful if you foresee some beneficiaries needing more financial assistance over a longer period of time. A trust will also protect your estate from third parties who may have a claim against one of your beneficiaries.

However, trusts are unnecessary because your gifts to beneficiaries under 18 (or if you prefer 21) will be controlled by your executor and then guardian after probate. This is possible because of the Uniform Gifts to Minors Act. While still allowing the guardian to use the funds in necessary situations, this act eliminates the need for a trust unless you perhaps have beneficiaries that are disabled, beneficiaries from a prior marriage, or if you have a large estate. Thus, a trust is worth the further complication if you wish for a guardian to spend more money on one child than another (ie: a child with special needs).

Do you want a trust?

☐   Yes   ☐   No

If yes, would this be:

☐ One trust for the benefit of all beneficiaries ("pooled" trust)

☐ Individual trusts for each of the beneficiaries

At what age do you want your beneficiaries to be when the trust ends?

☐ 18

☐ 21

☐ Other _____

Name of Trustee (please indicate below, along with his or her relationship to you):

1st Choice: _____

2nd Choice: _____

3rd Choice: _____

Do you want the trustee to have the power to dissolve the trust if it becomes unfeasible to maintain?

☐ Yes (note: the inherited property will remain under the guardian's control if the child is a minor at the time of the trust's termination)

☐ No

Do you want the trustee to exercise the power to terminate the trust if it falls below a specific amount?

☐ Yes   ☐ No

If yes, then what amount? $ _____

——————— ℘ Disinheriting Someone ℞ ———————

Do you wish to disinherit someone other than your spouse?

☐ Yes   ☐ No

If so, please indicate who as well as his or her relationship to you:

_____

Do you wish to disinherit anyone who contests your will?

☐ Yes ☐ No

Do you wish to have your executor distribute your estate, either outright or in trust, if you chose to disinherit your spouse? This may minimize any "right of election" that your spouse may have under the laws of jurisdiction.

☐ Yes ☐ No

Please note that some states provide a spouse a "right of election," which would grant him or her to apply the state law instead of what you wish in your will.

℘ Distribution of Estate to Children ℘

Do you wish for minor's gifts to be:

☐ Paid at the election of the executor

☐ Held in trust until the child reaches legal age

If you have adopted or stepchildren do you:

☐ Include them in your will the same as your natural children

☐ Exclude them from your will

☐ Have the will remain silent in regards to adopted and stepchildren

Do you have a child who is adopted or a stepchild?

☐ Yes ☐ No

Please name: _____

How do you wish for him or her to be treated in your will?

_____

_____

Please list all the names of your children:

_____

_____

_____

_____ ❦ Primary Beneficiaries ❧ _____

Whom do you wish to receive all or the majority of your estate?

☐ My spouse, if he or she survives me, and if not, then my children

☐ Disinherit spouse (to the fullest extent of the law)

☐ My children

☐ My parents in equal shares, or if not, then my siblings in equal shares

   Please list names and relationships

   _____

   _____

☐ To these beneficiaries (list name, relationship, and estate percentage)

   _____

   _____

If, for some reason, any of the before mentioned beneficiaries die before you and leave descendents, do you want the share of the deceased beneficiary to pass to their children or would you like your estate to pass only to the beneficiaries named above?

☐   Allow estate to pass to the children of any deceased beneficiary

☐   Allow estate to only pass to the named beneficiaries listed

If, for some reason, all your named beneficiaries either die before you or die within 30 days after you, please list those to whom you wish to leave your estate. Remember to provide his or her name, relationship, and percentage of your estate that you wish to lave them.

_____

_____

_____

_____ ℘ Living Will and Health Care ℞_____

Though a living will is a separate document from your will, it may be an important part of your estate plan. The living will provides instructions for your family and executor on what to do if you suffer an incurable medical condition or if you become incapacitated. This document directs doctors on how to care for you. You can provide specific details in your will to indicate the specific conditions that need to occur to activate it. Remember, once you activate it, it is in effect until you revoke it, which you can do at any time by either telling someone who can testify that you wanted to revoke it or by physically destroying it. However, this document only addresses continued life support if you have a terminable condition. For other situations, you will need a power of attorney for health care.

Do you want a living will?

☐ Yes   ☐ No

Another separate document, though equally important, is a special power of attorney that you grant for health care. You may execute this power of attorney in addition to or in lieu of your living will. It will appoint someone that you designate to make any medical care decisions for you if you are incapable of making your own decisions. This document provides for more situations than a living will. This will grant your power of attorney to make medical decisions on your behalf and also will allow him or her access to your medical record in order to make those decisions.

Do you want a health care power of attorney?

　　☐　Yes　　☐ No

Do you want your spouse to act as your agent if he or she is alive?

　　☐　Yes　　☐ No

If you do not wish for your spouse to act as your agent, please provide the name and address of the person that you wish to grant medical power of attorney to:

_____

Do you wish to donate your organs for transplant once you die? Please note that this information can often be found on your driver's license as well.

　　☐　Yes　　☐ No

If you answered yes, are you also willing to donate your organs for medical, educational, or scientific purposes?

　　☐　Yes　　☐ No

Would you prefer to die at home rather than in the hospital assuming that this does not place a burden upon your family?

　　☐　Yes　　☐ No

ℰ Springing Durable General Power of Attorney ℛ

While your will allows you control of the distribution of your property after you die, you are in control of your property while you are alive as long as you are of sound mind. However, if for some reason you become incapacitated, a court may revoke your right to manage your own affairs and grant the right to a guardian that the court appoints. You can appoint your own agent instead of the court's by granting someone you trust power of attorney.

A power of attorney authorizes another person to make decisions and act on your behalf. While a normal power of attorney becomes null and void when you are deemed mentally disabled, a springing durable power of attorney would actually take effect at this time. This power of attorney would last as long as you are alive or until you chose to revoke it. However, remember to name someone your attorney in fact because your power of attorney will have a strong authority over your affairs and while he or she may use it effectively, this power is also easily abused.

Would you like to have a springing durable power of attorney?

☐ Yes   ☐ No

Would you like your spouse to act as your agent?

☐ Yes   ☐ No

If you elect someone other than your spouse to act on your behalf, please list his or her name and his or her relationship to you below:

ℰ Funeral Arrangements ℛ

Perhaps you have an idea of how you wish your funeral to be performed.

It is essential to communicate your wishes with your family and friends prior to your death, because if you keep your wishes detailed in a letter of instruction that accompanies your will, these instructions may not be read until after your burial.

At my death I would like:

☐ To be cremated

☐ To have my body donated for scientific or medical purposes

☐ To be buried at a specific grave site or location (Please list below)

_____

☐ To be buried at sea

☐ To be buried with full military honors (Please also select another option in addition to this one)

☐ Other: _____

☐ I would prefer this decision to be made by those who survive me

_____ ✄ Your Financial Data ⚕_____

Please keep in mind that if your estate exceeds $1 million total that you may be subject to estate taxes and should consult your attorney.

1.) Determining the Value of Your Assets:

Please provide the numerical values in the chart. You only need to provide approximate figures if you do not know the actual value of your assets. Make sure that you have proof of ownership for any property requiring such.

	Joint	You	Spouse	Total
Checking Accounts				
Savings Accounts				
Money Market Accounts				
Stocks				
Bonds				
Mutual Funds				
Residence Equity				
Other Real Estate Equity				
Investments (Including Retirement)				
Closely-held Businesses				
Life Insurance				
Vehicles				
Furniture				
Jewelry				
Artwork & Antiques				
Electronics				
Other Personal Property				
Other Assets				
Other Assets				
Other Assets				
Other Assets				
Total				

In the past, have you ever filed an IRS Form 709 "A U.S. Gift Tax Return."

☐ Yes (please provide copy) ☐ No

2. Residence Information

A.) Primary Residence. Please list your address below:

_____

_____

Estimated Value	Amount of Mortgages	Equity	Monthly Mortgage Payment	Owned By

Please provide a copy of the deed and mortgages to allow for an expedited disbursement.

Original Purchase Price: $ _____

Cost of Additional Improvements: $ _____

How long do you plan on remaining at this residence? _____

What do you plan on doing with the property? _____

_____

B.) Secondary Residence. Please list your address below:

_____

_____

Estimated Value	Amount of Mortgages	Equity	Monthly Mortgage Payment	Owned By

Please provide a copy of the deed and mortgages to allow for an expedited disbursement.

Original Purchase Price: $ _____

Cost of Additional Improvements: $ _____

How long do you plan on keeping this residence? _____

What do you plan on doing with the property? _____

_____

Do you rent this residence?

☐ Yes ☐ No

3. Investment Account Information, not including retirement accounts

A.) **Jointly owned investment accounts** in your and your spouse's name

Location	Estimated Value	Amount of Margin Loans	Net Value	Other Co-Owners
Total				

B.) Investment accounts that you alone own:

Location	Estimated Value	Amount of Margin Loans	Net Value	Other Co-Owners
Total				

C.) Investment accounts that only your spouse owns:

Location	Estimated Value	Amount of Margin Loans	Net Value	Other Co-Owners
Total				

4.) Retirement Benefits

A.) List your retirement benefits:

Description	Current Value	Beneficiary
Total		

B.) List your spouse's retirement benefits:

Description	Current Value	Beneficiary
Total		

C.) Provide any other pertinent retirement account information:

_____

_____

5.) *Liability Information:*

A.) Joint Liabilities:

Creditor	Liability Amount	Payment Amount	Payment Frequency	Secured
Total				

B.) Your sole liabilities, other than previously listed:

Creditor	Liability Amount	Payment Amount	Payment Frequency	Secured
Total				

C.) Your spouse's liabilities, other than those previously listed:

Creditor	Liability Amount	Payment Amount	Payment Frequency	Secured
Total				

6.) Life Insurance Information:

A.) Life Insurance Policies (Please list both yours and your spouse's):

Company	Type	Face Amount (Death Benefit)	Cash Surrender Value	Beneficiary
Total				

B.) List only your life insurance policies:

Company	Type	Face Amount (Death Benefit)	Cash Surrender Value	Beneficiary
Total				

C.) List only your spouse's life insurance policies:

Company	Type	Face Amount (Death Benefit)	Cash Surrender Value	Beneficiary
Total				

D.) Please list any other vital information concerning you or your spouse's life insurance policies that may be helpful to your executor:

_____

_____

_____

TENTATIVE TAX

The tax base is the sum of the taxable estate and the adjusted taxable gifts, which are taxable gifts made after 1976. The tentative tax is then calculated by applying the following tax rates.

Amount	Tax
<$10,000	18%
$10,000 - $20,000	$1,800 + 20% of excess over $10,000
$20,001 - $40,000	$3,800 + 22% of excess over $20,000
$40,001 - $60,000	$8,200 + 24% of excess over $40,000
$60,001 - $80,000	$13,000 + 26% of excess over $60,000
$80,001 - $100,000	$18,200 + 28% of excess over $80,000
$100,001 - $150,000	$23,800 + 30% of excess over $100,000
$150,001 - $250,000	$38,800 + 32% of excess over $150,000
$250,001 - $500,000	$70,800 + 34% of excess over $250,000
$500,001 - $750,000	$155,800 + 27% of excess over $500,000
$750,001 - $1,000,000	$248,300 + 39% of excess over $750,000

RESOURCES

- http://www.investorguide.com/igu-article-159-planning-your-estate-the-importance-of-estate-planning-and-determining-your-net-worth.html

- http://www.lawguru.com/articles/showarticle.php?id=38

- http://msucares.com/pubs/publications/p1742.pdf

- http://www.investorguide.com/igu-subject-23-estate-planning.html

- http://ria.thomson.com/EstatePlanning/

- http://trusts-estates.lawyers.com/estate-planning/

AUTHOR BIOGRAPHY AND DEDICATION

To my husband and children, who have helped me to create the life I've dreamed of living.

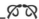

Sandy Baker is the mother of three and the wife of an amazing man. Together they provide a range of helpful tools to help others to make their dreams and wishes come true. Estate planning is part of the tools that Sandy helps to present to others as a method of enriching their lives through leaving their legacy. With many years of professional writing experience, namely as a ghostwriter, she's written and researched the topic for many years, enhancing her ability to provide a thorough book for readers.

GLOSSARY

If there is anything that is true about estate planning, it is the many different terms that are often confusing. Here are some that you need to take note of. These are simple, brief definitions of some terms you will find in this book. Make sure you consider that there may be differences in how they are used.

529 PLAN A 529 Plan is a tax free investment in which a person can donate $12,000 a year to fund a child's higher education expenses.

A

AB TRUST An AB Trust is one that establishes two trusts, one for each spouse. The surviving spouse can then use the property in the other's trust, but avoids double taxation on the property from when one spouse dies to when the second spouse dies.

ABATEMENT This is the process of pulling back specific gifts under a will when it becomes necessary to create a fund to meet expenses or to pay taxes, or in other specific situations.

ABSTRACT OF TRUST This tool allows you to say that your trust exists and that it will be used. It is a "short list" of what is included in that trust, rather than spelling it all out.

ADEMPTION In ademption statues, laws are in place which protect heirs that do not or cannot receive what you leave to them in your will. If you leave property in your will and estate to someone and that property is no longer part of your estate, this statute defines what should happen.

ANNUAL EXEMPTION This is the amount of money a person can give away each year tax free.

B

BASIS The tax basis is the value that is assigned to the property from which taxable gain or loss on a sale is determined. This means that when property is purchased, its basis is usually the cost.

BENEFICIARY A beneficiary is someone or a group that benefits from the gifts made under a legal document, which can include wills, trusts, pay on death accounts, retirement plans, and insurance products. This is the person that gets something from these documents.

C

CHARITABLE REMAINDER TRUST This is a type of trust in which an irrevocable gift of property is made to a tax free charity.

CHILD'S TRUST A trust that is created solely for the use of one child who is a minor.

COMMUNITY PROPERTY Property that is shared between you and your spouse, in a community living state. This property belongs equally to both parties as it was obtained during the marriage.

COVERDELL ACCOUNT This is a type of account that allows a person to contribute $2,000 a year to a beneficiary's education.

CREDITOR A company or an organization that is owed money; this is the company that lent you money that you need to repay.

CUSTODIAN Under the Uniform Transfers to Minor Act, this is the person named by you to care for the property that is left to a minor child.

D

DEATH TAXES Death taxes, probate taxes, or estate taxes are taxes that are assessed on the property of a person that has died.

DURABLE POWER OF ATTORNEY The power of attorney which remains effective even when the principal (person that created it) becomes incapacitate. This person is authorized to act in the other's place and is called an attorney in fact.

E

ELECTRONIC WILL This is simply a will composed on a computer.

ENDING CLAUSE The ending clause is the part of the will where the person and the witnesses sign.

ESTATE All the property that you own when you die is your estate. There are various ways of determining the value of your estate, as defined in this book, including your probate estate and your taxable estate.

ESTATE PLANNING Planning for what will happen to your estate when you die while you are still alive. It helps you move your estate from your property to that of your heirs in the best manner possible.

ESTATE RECOVERY ACT This is a law that provides for repayment of Medicaid benefits for certain individuals.

ESTATE TAXES These are taxes that are applied to your property when you die. There are various tax situations that you could be in; for example, the federal estate tax is levied when a person reaches the estate tax threshold for the year that they die.

ESTATE TAX THRESHOLD The dollar amount, as defined by the federal government, for the year that you die, at which point taxes are levied on your estate.

ETHICAL WILL This type of will is a separate document from the legal will in which a person can express his or her feelings, thoughts, concerns, and values.

EXECUTOR The individual that will manage your estate, move through probate, and collect all your assets. He or she will distribute them to your heirs as you define in your will.

F

FAMILY POT TRUST This is a type of trust in which all the property is left to all children and can then be used in any amount by each of the children.

FINAL BENEFICIARIES Those people that will receive property from your estate.

G

GENERATION SKIPPING TRUST This is a trust that is set up to avoid double taxation. The principal leaves the trust for the grandchild rather than for their children. This helps to avoid taxation from the principal to the child and then again from the taxation when the child passes it to the grandchild.

GIFTS Property that is given to another person or organization. This can be done throughout life or through trusts, wills, and a living trust after death.

GIFT TAXES Taxes that are levied on any gifts when the gifts are given (usually before death).

GIVING CLAUSE This is the part of the will that bequeaths a person's belongings to his or her heirs.

GRANTOR A grantor is a person that establishes a trust.

H

HANDWRITTEN WILL A handwritten will is simply one written by hand; it is also know as a holographic will.

HEALTH CARE DIRECTIVE This document will define the wishes of the document writer in regards to health care when they cannot communicate those wishes themselves. It names a person that will make decisions for them at this time.

HEIRS Those that will inherit property, by law, at the time of death of those they are related to. Heirs will receive property that is not left specifically through a will or trust to someone else.

I

INHERITANCE TAXES Taxes that are imposed on property that is received by heirs at the time of death.

INSURANCE A product that is purchased that provides protection from a variety of situations in the event that they happen. Life insurance, for example, provides coverage in a monetary benefit if the insured person dies while the policy is in effect.

INTANGIBLE PERSONAL PROPERTY This is any type of property that is financially oriented.

INTESTACY This is the term for a will that is legally invalid.

IRREVOCABLE TRUST A trust that can no longer be changed.

J

JOINT TENANCY When two or more people own property, the other will become the owner of the entire property when one dies.

JOINT WILL A joint will is a single document that represents the wishes of two people.

L

LIFE BENEFICIARY This inclusion in an AB Trust allows for the other spouse to take use of the property in Trust A for his own needs, when one spouse dies. It does not provide ownership of this property to the spouse, though, which is the key factor in avoiding estate taxes.

LIFE INSURANCE TRUST This trust is one that owns a life insurance policy. It helps to reduce the size of the original owner's taxable estate.

LIMITED LIABILITY COMPANY (LLC) An LLC is a category of business that allows the owners to be taxed as a partnership but with the limited liability of a corporation.

LIMITED LIABILITY PARTNERSHIP This is a type of company organization, now available in most states, that offers advantages of both the partnership and incorporation styles.

LIVING TRUST A living trust is set up while the person is still alive, which still allows them to control what is in the trust until they die. It helps to minimize the value of property that ends up going through probate. Grantors are able to specify that the property in the trust will pass right to the beneficiaries at the time of death, avoiding probate.

M

MARITAL DEDUCTION In accordance with tax law, a marital deduction allows all property that is passed from one spouse to the other spouse at the time of death to be free from taxes.

MARITAL EXEMPTION This is the law that allows any gift given to one's spouse to be tax free.

MUTUAL WILL A mutual will is a document in which two people's wills or estate plans are linked together.

N

NUNCUPATIVE WILL A nuncupative will is a spoken will often used when a person is on his or her deathbed.

O

OPENING CLAUSE An opening clause is a clause in a will that identifies the person, establishes free will, and introduces those included in the will.

P

PARTIAL INTESTACY This is the term used when a will is present but may not be legally binding or may have a missing clause.

PAY ON DEATH Variety of methods that are used for the payment of funds at the time of death. It defines who will acquire what remains in the account when the holder of the account dies.

PERSONAL PROPERTY CLAUSE This is a clause in a will that dictates what will happen to a person's personal items.

POWER OF ATTORNEY The power of attorney provides legal documentation that the individual is giving authorization for someone other than themselves to act for them.

PROBATE Probate is a process that includes several steps. Probate will authenticate the will of the deceased, appoints the executor or administrator of your will, pays debts and taxes that are due on the estate, identifies who the heirs of the estate are, and distributes the property in the will to those that are designated in the will.

PROPERTY GUARDIAN A property guardian is the person in charge of the property a person gives to his or her children until the children reach the age of 18.

Q

QTIP TRUST A Qualified Terminable Interest Property Trust is a trust that does not reduce or stop estate taxes, but it does postpone them. It can be used when an individual estate exceeds the estate tax threshold to postpone the payment of taxes on the estate.

R

REAL PROPERTY Real property is all land and all buildings attached to it, as well as all improvements made to it. It is real estate. Anything that is not real property is considered to be personal property.

REAL PROPERTY CLAUSE This clause is the part of the will that dictates how a person's property is to be divided or to whom it is bequeathed.

REMAINDERMAN The remainderman is the individual that receives what is left in the trust after the income beneficiaries receive their portion of the trust.

RESIDUAL BENEFICIARY A person that will receive property that is left in a will or trust that is not given to others in that document. It can also mean a person that receives property from a trust when the life beneficiary dies.

RESIDUARY CLAUSE A residuary clause is the part of the will that determines who gets the items not listed in the document.

RIGHT OF SURVIVORSHIP When two people own property, this is the right that the joint tenant has in claiming the other's share of the property at the time of death.

S

SIMPLE WILL This type of will consists of a single piece of documentation that describes a person's wishes.

STATUTORY WILL This is a type of will in which the person fills in the blanks and is unable to customize the document.

SUCCESSOR TRUSTEE A successor trustee is a person that the creator of the trust places in charge when they die, if they are the trustee of the living trust.

T

TANGIBLE PERSONAL PROPERTY This is any type of property that can be touched.

TAX CLAUSE The tax clause is the part of a will that identifies a person's tax strategy and how he or she wishes taxes to be paid on the estate.

TAXABLE ESTATE This is the value of the estate that is able to be taxed, as it goes over the estate tax threshold or the allowable amount of no taxing.

TENANCY BY THE ENTIRETY This form of tenancy is one that is a form of marital property ownership. It provides joint ownership of property to both spouses.

TERM LIFE INSURANCE This is a type of life insurance policy that is for a specific length of time and that carries no cash value while the insured is alive.

TESTACY This is the term for a will that is legally valid.

TRUST A trust is a legal document and situation in which the grantor or trustor places property into the trust that is managed by the trustee until it passes to the beneficiary.

TRUSTEE The trustee of a trust is the person that will manage the trust for the beneficiary until they can take claim to the property in it.

U

UMBRELLA LIABILITY Umbrella liability is an insurance policy that provides additional coverage for any claim filed against a person.

UNIFORM SIMULTANEOUS DEATH ACT This is a law used when there is a need to determine who died first; most often, it is assumed that each spouse survived the other.

UNIFORM TRANSFERS TO MINORS ACT This law provides for the method that property is transferred to minors in the event of a death.

UNIVERSAL LIFE INSURANCE This is an insurance plan in which the insured renews the policy yearly and in which there is a return on investment.

V

VARIABLE LIFE INSURANCE A type of life insurance plan that allows the insured to invest in a pre-selected stock, bond, or money market; the success of this investment determines the value of the policy.

VIDEO WILL A video will is a visual recording of your will; this cannot be a person's only way of communicating his or her wishes.

W

WHOLE LIFE INSURANCE This is an insurance plan in which the insured is covered for life and in which a portion of the payment is deposited into an interest-earning account.

WILL A will is a legal document that defines what the deceased person's wishes are in regard to his or her property. It provides for what their intentions are for where property should go after they die.

INDEX

J

L

M

O

P